MARDUKITE MASTER COURSE
ACADEMY LECTURES
VOL. 4

MARDUKITE
SYSTEMOLOGY

Titles in this series by Joshua Free:
Vol.1 – Magick & Mysticism
Vol.2 – Druids, Elves & Dragons
Vol.3 – Mesopotamian Tradition
Vol.4 – Mardukite Systemology

Mardukite Research Library Catlogue No. "MMC-3S"

Based on the Lectures by Joshua Free for the
Mardukite Master Course given during September 2020
excerpted from *The Complete Mardukite Master Course*

Every effort has been given to match wording and inflection for lecture transcripts based on the recordings made by Mardukite Academy of Systemology

Published from
Mardukite Borsippa HQ, San Luis Valley, Colorado

cum superiorum privilegio veniaque

The Founding Church of Mardukite Zuism,
Mardukite Academy & Systemology Society

MARDUKITE ACADEMY – COLLECTOR'S EDITION

MARDUKITE MASTER COURSE
ACADEMY LECTURES
VOL. 4

MARDUKITE SYSTEMOLOGY

Based on the Lectures
by Joshua Free

THE JOSHUA FREE IMPRINT
JFI PUBLICATIONS

© 2022, JOSHUA FREE

ISBN : 979-8-9864379-2-7

No part of this publication may be reproduced in any form or by any means, electronic or mechanical, including photocopying, recording, or any information storage or retrieval system, without permission from the publisher. This book is not intended to substitute medical treatment or professional advice.

The Mardukite Academy Lectures given during September 2020 for Academy Grade-III of the Mardukite Master Course regarding Mardukite Systemology.

Mardukite Academy Collector's Edition—*July 2022*
mardukite.com

The _Original_ Master Course Lectures

Commemorating his silver anniversary and drawing from 25 years of experiential esoteric research and underground literary developments, world-renowned mystic philosopher and prodigious occult author, Joshua Free, provides the professional qualifications necessary for "mastering" upper-level understanding of his collected works in the same way that an artist "masters" their craft. Nothing is held back in this surprisingly candid presentation of materials.

This is volume four of a four-part series, providing a serious Seeker with full transcripts to 13 of the 48 Academy Lectures previously published in the mega-anthology "Complete Mardukite Master Course."

Here you will find an insightful tome demonstrating a refreshing approach to understanding Ascension and Mardukite Systemology in the 21st century.

Although recent years have seen an advancement in the work, all publications by Joshua Free, written and published between 1995 and 2019, pertain to a singular continuum of complete instruction divided into three knowledge tiers or "Grades." A complete library collection of all "core material" described in the "Mardukite Master Course" was also reissued in four different Master Edition textbooks: "The Great Magickal Arcanum," "Merlyn's Complete Book of Druidism," "Necronomicon: The Complete Anunnaki Legacy" and "The Systemology Handbook" – totaling 3,600 pages in all.

Now YOU can experience the legendary "Master Course" from anywhere in the Universe, exactly as given in-person by Joshua Free to the "Mardukite Academy of Systemology" in September 2020.

THE GRADE-III ACADEMY LECTURES

INTRODUCTIONS

Introducing the Mardukite Master Course . . . 9
Materials of the Mardukite Master Course . . . 17
Mardukite Master Course Training Schedule . . . 19
Introducing Mardukite Grade-III Materials . . . 21

THE ACADEMY LECTURES (GRADE-III)

1—36. The Tablets of Destiny (*Sept. 28, 2020*) . . . 24
2—37. Mardukite Systemology (*Sept. 28, 2020*) . . . 40
3—38. Grade-III Defined (*Sept. 28, 2020*) . . . 55
4—39. The Original Thesis (*Sept. 28, 2020*) . . . 71
5—40. The Standard Model (*Sept. 28, 2020*) . . . 87
6—41. Systemology Handbook (*Sept. 29, 2020*) . . . 107
7—42. Master Control (*Sept. 29, 2020*) . . . 122
8—43. Commanding the Mind (*Sept. 29, 2020*) . . . 137
9—44. Beta-Defragmentation (*Sept. 29, 2020*) . . . 153
10—45. Crystal Clear (*Sept. 30, 2020*) . . . 169
11—46. Awareness Tech (*Sept. 30, 2020*) . . . 185
12—47. Actualization Tech (*Sept. 30, 2020*) . . . 200
13—48. Graduation, Final Lecture (*Sept. 30, 2020*) . . . 217

APPENDIX

Suggested Reading and Additional Materials . . . 233

INTRODUCING THE
MARDUKITE MASTER COURSE

The single most purpose of our *Mardukite Master Course* is to ensure, certify and provide professional qualifications for "mastering" an understanding of the materials in the same way that an artist "masters" their craft. The complete *Mardukite Master Course* spans three *Grades* of knowledge and is given only to those *Seekers* that first properly worked through all three *Grades*, and may then be rightfully considered *Masters* of this knowledge. Extents of such "mastery" should prove readily obvious (objectively), lending to increased qualities of *Self-Actualization*, personal leadership and the certainty to manage and instruct *Mardukite Groups*.

Current works available by Joshua Free—written and published between 1995 and 2019—all pertain to a singular stream of complete instruction that is divided into three *Grades* or knowledge tiers. The *Mardukite Master Course* is intended to grant a clear unification of material presented across all three *Grades* under the banner of "Mardukite Systemology," which is also the name given to *Grade-III*. The two are interconnected (*Grade-III* and the *Master Course*); hence the complete *Mardukite Master Course* is only delivered to *Seekers* at the completion of *Grade-III*. There are "higher" *Grades* within the domain of "NexGen Systemology," but the *Mardukite Master Course* successfully covers all specifically "Mardukite Master" *Grades*: I, II and III.

It is important to clarify what we mean by *Grades* and distinguish the materials that pertain to each. In most instances, instruction for these *Grades*—as delivered in the materials (books) over the past 25 years—was all self-administered; meaning it has been explored independent of properly structured groups or trained instructors. In the past, *Seekers* selected a volume at random, had at it on their own for a while, then walked away with whatever level of understanding might be attained, even if severely fragmented. Most are unaware that the works—no matter the theme—are all tied together. They are divided as follows:

GRADE-I	Western Magical Tradition ("Magick")
GRADE-II	Ancient Mystery School of Mesopotamia
GRADE-III	Futurist/NexGen Mardukite Systemology

It can be said that the *Grades* are all a part of a single continuum—one which is explored in a "reverse engineering" style in order to provide the greatest certainty for effective workable future applications that will advance the spiritual evolution of the *Human Condition*, particularly the *Self* that is participating in and experiencing a co-creation of the Physical Universe and a continued existence of its conditions. As a single continuum, the *Grades* do actually overlap on many points—and often times these "bridges" between levels of understanding are what we are highlighting profusely for our *Mardukite Master Course*. This preferred approach—treating the universal knowledge and its records as a single wholeness rather than an emphasis on individual parts—developed after many years of experiment and discovery.

Direction of the *Mardukite Master Course* loosely follows a chronological pathway charted by Joshua Free from 1995 through 2019—meaning: from the release of the first "Merlyn Stone" *Grade-I* discourses on "magick" and "Druidism" until the recent completion of *Grade-III* as "Mardukite Systemology." Between these *Grades*, a *Seeker* discovers abundant source material known as the "Mardukite Core" comprising *Grade-II*. These *Grades* also loosely follow a premise for organization set out in the 1990's for *Grade-I* Alumni of "Merlyn Stone's School of Magick"* that is referred to elsewhere as "The Sacred Order of the Crystal Dawn." The outline for this premise in 1999 proposed the structuring of "A New Illuminati" using the work published by Joshua Free over the next two decades.

---

* Also operating 1998-2000 as "The Elven Fellowship Circle of Magick" in Denver.

There are no strictly enforced "title-badges" and/or "initiations" defining *Grades* when applied to individual *Mardukite Groups* (outside the religious organizational function of *Mardukite Zuism* specifically) for "study" or "instructive" purposes. A *Master* may choose to adopt a particular regimen for their *Seekers* as applicable to each *Grade* and in alignment with the theme and goals of the group. Starting with the original *Grade-I* "Merlyn Stone" volume by Joshua Free—THE SORCERER'S HANDBOOK—reissued for its 21st Anniversary as a collector's edition hardcover, sufficient material is now available in each "core" toward defining group structure as it pertains to the greater "*whole*" at each *Grade*.

Parameters assigned to formal progressive *Grades* are approximately equivalent to the *first three* "*degrees*" of the "Crystal Dawn" program; which is the extent an individual "Chapter" or "Lodge" is allowed to administer (apart from authority of a "Grand Lodge"). For two decades, this clause permitted a *Master* of the *Third Degree* to launch a "Chapter" or "Group" as an official extension of the organization; so long as the *Seeker* had completed the *Master Course*. However, no such *Grade-III* materials were sufficiently supplied as a "core" until 2019 to make this possible.

The basic pattern of development across the *Grades* follows progressive and cumulative ascent up the "Ladder of Lights" or "Gateways to Infinity" first described by the Ancient Mystery School of Mesopotamia as a sevenfold "Babylonian Stargate" system. The chronology of the *Grades* begins with the most apparent and recent influences of the contemporary "New Age"; meaning the modern communication and conception of "magick" and metaphysics—otherwise known as the Western Magical Tradition, which maintained its popularity for the past several thousand years in Europe. This is the essence of *Grade-I*, which is essentially the "*Lunar Gate.*"

A *Seeker* exploring origins behind magickal correspondences, practices, ceremonies and ritualism of various European developments—including everything from ancient Celtic Druids to more modern esoteric Hermetic Orders—will at one juncture or another intersect with the even older Ancient Mystery School present in Mesopotamia —systematized in "Mardukite Babylon" at the inception of the *Age of Aries* (c. 2160 B.C.)—an extension of the former loosely organized Sumerian civilization, now collectively making up *Grade-II* and the key to open the "*Nabu Gate.*"

When a *Seeker* considers this logical progression: we begin with what is most readily familiar and accessible at *Grade-I*, loading the shot in the sling, and then pulling back to the extent that we may be certain, by examining the oldest literary records in *Grade-II*; the very basis for which our *Grade-I* material is actually based, albeit forgotten to the sands of time coupled with thousands of years of programming and encoding separating the two. History and tradition begins with "writing," and so we cannot be certain of anything further than what we have actual accounts of; yet still we find that these *Arcane Tablets* provide an understanding that is milestones beyond what is demonstrated in contemporary society today.

There are many ways of which we can demonstrate how the knowledge between these two *Grades* is bridged and overlaps in application and study; but the *Grades* are distinguished as they are for good reason—and we are not to muddy the waters of a *Seeker's* thinking by incorporating unnecessary complications to instruction. A line has been drawn, if only even from necessity, between the *Grades* by using the *Mardukite Chamberlains Grade-II* material as a benchmark for our evaluation of other materials.

Essentially—all volumes by Joshua Free pertaining exclusively to ancient Mesopotamia are considered *Grade-II*; all volumes pertaining to general mysticism, magick, esoterica, Druidism, &tc are considered *Grade-I*. This is not to say that "higher realizations" are inaccessible from lower *Grade* materials, nor is there a guarantee that "higher realizations" are gleaned directly from reading higher *Grade* materials. A *Seeker* working through the entirety of the first two *Grades* may reach all necessary "ledges" of "knowing" on their own merit, independent of outside instruction. But given that only one-way communication relay takes place from this book-learning, there is no guarantee that an individual will correctly gauge the distance between "ledges" of "knowing" on their ascent up as they leap about unaided.

An early premise of "higher" *Grades* comprised an ORIGINAL THESIS for a new flavor of "New Thought" provided exclusively to *Grade-II* Mardukite Alumni in 2011 as "NexGen Systemology." The official "Core" of *Grade-III* was not released to the public by Joshua Free until late 2019 as "Mardukite Systemology." It is from the vantage point of *Grade-III*, and a mastery of that same tier of knowledge, that we actually treat all of which the *Mardukite Master Course* represents. Although a *Seeker* could certainly remain at one or another *Grade*, an individual must demonstrate total understanding of all three *Grades* to be officially considered a *Master*.

Earliest contributions toward this *Course* from the 1990's are considered *Grade-I*, pertaining to practical magick, general metaphysics, the Western Magical Tradition and its archetypal scions, the *Druids*. The original *Grade-I* volumes pertaining to magick and metaphysics are THE SORCERER'S HANDBOOK and ARCANUM by Joshua Free. In addition to THE DRUID'S HANDBOOK, there are two volumes that both complete the *Druid Cycle* and effectively "bridge" to *Grade-II* elements that incorporate Mesopotamia: DRACONOMICON and ELVENOMICON.[*]

A *Seeker* working through the original *Grade-I* "Handbooks" may also choose to take an alternate "bridge" between the ritualism and ceremonialism of *Grade-I* with *Grade-II*, as des-

---

[*] *"Elvenomicon"* formerly released as *"Book of Elven-Faerie"* (from 2004 to 2018) by Joshua Free.

cribed in THE VAMPYRE'S HANDBOOK by Joshua Free.* The original 2015 release of these materials for *Moroii ad Vitam Paramus* served as a contemporary "holding point" for Alumni after the completion of *Grade-II* work, while a "Core" for *Grade-III* developed behind-the-scenes until late 2019. For our purposes, this now means that there are several "entry" points for a *Seeker* to experience glamour and enchantment of the *Grade-I* "Lunar Gate" on the way to higher avenues of *Self-Actualization*—which is the ultimate goal behind the *Master* level.

In 2008, existing ARCANUM and ELVENOMICON materials contributed to the establishment of *Mardukite Ministries*, an underground umbrella organization that took control of the former "Merlyn Stone" legacy of Joshua Free as a "ledge" for developing *Grade-II*. By 2009, the *Mardukite Chamberlains* emerged—a global network contributing to progressive generation and dissemination of a "Mardukite Core" of materials, providing the inception of the modern "Mardukite" (and "Mardukite Zuism") paradigms. This living spiritual philosophy dispensed at *Grade-II* is drawn heavily from the ancient cuneiform tablet records of Mesopotamia/Babylon.

Mardukite Chamberlains participated in developing the bulk of material for *Grade-II* from 2009 through 2011. These materials were simultaneously presented in two guises—the *same* materials, but dispensed in two different formats: one emphasizing the *Anunnaki Legacy* as a demonstration of more "academic" and "intellectual" pursuits into ancient history and its esoteric traditions; the other, emphasizing the title of the NECRONOMICON due to the high correlation and association of "New Age" data regarding the ancient "Mardukite Babylonian" tradition. When treated in its entirety as the *Complete Anunnaki Legacy* from within the Mardukite paradigm, presentation of the two "formats" is essentially identical. *Grade-II* should not, however, be confu-

---

* *"The Vampyre's Handbook"* formerly released as *"Vampyre Magick"* by Joshua Free; an anthology edition containing *"Vampyre Bible"* and *"Cybernomicon."*

sed with *any* other outside treatment of the *"Necronomicon"* subject.

Starting in 2009, the original source book of *Grade-II* developed into an anthology composed from individual discourses produced for the *Mardukite Chamberlains* and compiled into NECRONOMICON: THE ANUNNAKI BIBLE. Then, over the next two years, several key elements were added to expand the source book; additionally, several volumes were added to the *Grade-II* core, including Joshua Free's GATES OF THE NECRONOMICON and NECRONOMICON: THE ANUNNAKI GRIMOIRE.[‡] These anthologies contain several stand-alone discourses in themselves—all of which were consolidated into a complete *Grade-II* mega-anthology titled NECRONOMICON: THE COMPLETE ANUNNAKI LEGACY (with a special *10th Anniversary Master Edition* released in early 2020).

The gradation (*Grades*) structure and concept of the *Mardukite Master Course* was announced in August 2019 at THE TABLETS OF DESTINY lectures, as described (from transcripts) in the *Grade-III* text of the same title:—

> "Some of you that have been really following along through the materials over the years already have an understanding, from the *Grades* previously provided... And this is one of the keys or secrets held by the *Master*—an individual who has a complete workable understanding of these various levels and degrees represented in former instruction, but they are not themselves formally attached to any of it—drawing up only those solid examples suitable for citation, example and demonstration. So, that's what a Master is, and we are referring now to this intermediary *Grade-III* 'Mardukite Systemology' material as the *Master*

[‡] *"Gates of the Necronomicon"* anthology includes *"The Sumerian Legacy"* and *"Necronomicon Revelations -or- Crossing to the Abyss"*; *"Necronomicon Grimoire"* anthology includes *"The Complete Book of Marduk by Nabu"* and *"The Maqlu Ritual Book."*

> *Grade*. I expect to also develop a formal instruction course for that, which will solidify the unification of the extant 'Mardukite Core' and NexGen Systemology for this Grade."—*Joshua Free*

The other significant portion of *Grade-III* material is found within the textbook for the CRYSTAL CLEAR Mardukite Systemology Self-Defragmentation Course Program developed by Joshua Free and officially released in December 2019, so as to make certain that proper introductory tools were available for the 2020's decade to usher in a *NexGen* evolution in consciousness. *Grade-III* emphasizes strengthening personal certainty and management of "Reality," employing spiritual philosophies of "Mardukite Systemology." This is our launch point for all further upper-level *Grades*, just as much as it is a capstone representing minimum requirements for our *Mardukite Master Course*—intended to treat all material of *Grades I*, *II* and *III*.

MATERIALS OF THE
MARDUKITE MASTER COURSE

Since 2009, materials comprising the *Mardukite Research Library* have included all officially published works by Joshua Free to date. From 2008 through 2018, management and responsibility of these materials fell upon the *Mardukite Truth Seeker Press* governed by *Mardukite Ministries* and maintained by the *Mardukite Chamberlains*. As of 2018, a consistent transfer of official responsibility for all materials is increasingly assumed by the *Joshua Free Publishing Imprint*.

Throughout the years, a continuous development ensued, contributing to the release of many materials—including both those mentioned previously in this introduction, and other supplemental works that have appeared or are reissued for posterity. As the work progressed, goals for refinement and consolidation of the knowledge were repeatedly observed in newer editions and publications. Up until recently, the work was exceptionally "fluid" and required considerable attention over the course of its development. Information and discourses were released as they were discovered or refined for many years before appearing as the newly revised "collected works" anthologies and other "collector's editions" in the past year—making the materials more accessible and comprehensible than ever before possible. Goal attained.

It is of benefit for the *Seeker* (and *Master-in-Training*) to see an outright listing of all available graded materials (and their supplements) considered for inclusion as the *Mardukite Master Course*. Titles given represent the most current editions at the time of preparing this introduction. Some *Seekers* may already be in possession of former editions of these materials; and while the titles may change—and volumes may be collected for various anthologies—any "*Liber*"* designations used to catalogue the *Mardukite Resear-*

---

* The term *Liber* (meaning *book*) is used by esoteric organizations to *ch Library* remain fixed to a particular discourse or release in perpetuity. This means, regardless of whatever "title" may be attached to, for example, *Liber-50* (or whatever anthology it may appear in), the material designated "*Liber-50*" is always *Liber-50*, in any of its formats or revisions. Although some *Seekers* have not taken note of these *liber designations,* this internal consistency has been maintained openly and publicly for over a decade.

---

title their work.

MARDUKITE MASTER COURSE TRAINING SCHEDULE

|| GRADE-I || ROUTE OF MAGICK & METAPHYSICS ||

Primary Textbooks:[∞]
        THE SORCERER'S HANDBOOK
        ARCANUM: GREAT MAGICAL ARACNUM
Supplementary:
Additional: *Route of Druidism & The Dragon Legacy*

|| GRADE-I || ROUTE OF DRUIDISM & THE DRAGON LEGACY ||

Primary Textbooks:[*]
        THE DRUID'S HANDBOOK (*Liber-D Series*)
        ELVENOMICON (*Liber-D Series*)
        DRACONOMICON (*Liber-D Series*)
Supplementary:
        THE VAMPYRE'S HANDBOOK
        --The Vampyre's Bible (*Liber V*)
        --Cybernomicon (*Liber V2*)
Optional: *Draconomicon Vol.2: The Pheryllt Researches*
Additional: *Route of Mesopotamian Mysteries*

|| GRADE-II || ROUTE OF MESOPOTAMIAN MYSTERIES ||

Primary Textbooks:[‡]
        NECRONOMICON: THE ANUNNAKI BIBLE
         (-or- THE COMPLETE ANUNNAKI BIBLE)
        --Mardukite Tablet Catalogue (*Liber-N,L,G,9*)
        --The Book of Sajaha-the-Seer (*Liber-S*)
        GATES OF THE NECRONOMICON
        --Sumerian Religion (*Liber-50*)
        --Babylonian Myth & Magic (*Liber-51+E*)

[∞] Grade-I, Route-A Anthology also available—*"The Great Magickal Arcanum"* (2020 Hardcover) by Joshua Free.

[*] Grade-I, Route-D Anthology also available—*"Merlyn's Complete Book of Druidism"* (Hardcover) by Joshua Free.

[‡] Grade-II Anthology also available—*"Necronomicon: The Complete Anunnaki Legacy"* (Hardcover) by Joshua Free.

--Necronomicon Revelations (*Liber-R*)
--Crossing to the Abyss (*Liber-555*)
NECRONOMICON: ANUNNAKI GRIMOIRE
  (-or- PRACTICAL BABYLONIAN MAGIC)
--Babylonian Magic (*Liber-E*)
--The Book of Marduk by Nabu (*Liber-W*)
--The Maqlu Ritual Book (*Liber-M*)
--Enochian Magician's Handbook (*Liber-K*)
Supplementary: Optnl: *The Anunnaki Tarot (Liber-T)*
Addnl: *Route of Mardukite Systemology*

|| GRADE-III || ROUTE OF MARDUKITE SYSTEMOLOGY ||

Primary Textbooks:[∞]
  THE TABLETS OF DESTINY (*Liber-One*)
  CRYSTAL CLEAR (*Liber-2B*)
Supplementary:
  SYSTEMOLOGY: ORIGINAL THESIS (*Liber-S-1X*)
  THE POWER OF ZU (*Liber-S-1Z*)
Optional: *Pantheisticon (300th Anniversary Edition)*
Additional: *Route of The Mardukite Master Course*
  Route of Professional Piloting (Grade-IV+)

[∞] Grade-III Anthology also available—*"The Systemology Handbook"* (Hardcover) by Joshua Free.

INTRODUCING MARDUKITE GRADE-III

Greetings fellow Truth Seekers!

Welcome to the *Mardukite Master Course* for *Grade-III* materials!

When a Seeker arrives at the *"Pathway to Self-Honesty"* represented by the *Grade-III* work—known as Mardukite Systemology—they are reaching for the highest state of knowing and being—reaching for total ultimate mastery of *Life, the Universe and Everything.* This is what former "Grades" and "Routes" of the *Mardukite Master Course* ultimately lead to; all of which, up to this point, are proven complimentary—and not necessarily exclusive—to one other. *Grade-III* is no different; although it may be alternately studied either as a finale to the former sequence of "Grades" or as a stand-alone entry point into "Mardukite/NexGen Systemology" and/or "Mardukite Zuism."

Our *Mardukite Master Course* work for *Grade-III "Route of Mardukite Systemology"* (and/or "NexGen Systemology") starts, of course, with a lot of reading. The two primary textbooks are THE TABLETS OF DESTINY: USING ANCIENT WISDOM TO UNLOCK HUMAN POTENTIAL (by Joshua Free) and its companion, CRYSTAL CLEAR: THE SELF-ACTUALIZATION MANUAL & GUIDE TO TOTAL AWARENESS.

These materials introduce practical applications of "Self-Processing"—a highly specialized former of directed focused attention on specific "associative thoughts" and "personal programming" that tend to restrict or limit the freedoms of the Spirit and its creative ability to maintain the highest optimum level of existence using the techniques or technology ("tech") of this specialized applied spiritual philosophy.

But...even with the straightforward nature of these textbooks, it is possible that a Seeker becomes overwhelmed by the introduction of this new advanced paradigm.

Although rudimentary by comparison, the materials contained within SYSTEMOLOGY: THE ORIGINAL THESIS were developed and released (underground to the *NexGen Systemology Society*) nearly a decade prior to the establishment of any true "textbook" from which to launch the subject—which is why THE TABLETS OF DESTINY is catalogued as "*Mardukite Systemology Liber-One*," as contrasted against a backdrop of the former "*Mardukite Chamberlains*" (*Grade-II*) research library. As a result, the fundamentals presented in SYSTEMOLOGY: THE ORIGINAL THESIS may be of incredible benefit to any Seeker that either is finding difficulties understanding the concepts presented in THE TABLETS OF DESTINY, or else is wanting a better understanding of how this information developed.

As an educational "route" toward esoteric mastery on an intellectual level, and as a personal "Pathway to Self-Honesty" for any determined *Seeker*, the combination of all that has "come before" (meaning that which encompasses the former "Grades") now converges toward a point of "higher level" understanding—a new "ledge" of "knowing" that is only partially gleaned by the average *Seeker* working their way through the previously graded mysteries:

Grade-I : a lunar-level of magic, enchantment and fantasy; and
Grade-II : a mercurian-level of hermetic wisdom and celestial philosophies.

Unlike *Grade-I* and *Grade-II*, where a *Seeker* may rely on supplemental historical records to validate accounts of "tradition" or "cultural systemology," the *Grade-III* futurist/NexGen "applied spiritual philosophy" ("tech") of Mardukite Systemology only partially leans on the former "occult" interpretations of teachings drawn from the Ancient Mystery School. *Grade-III*, quite simply, represents the premium advancement and logical "next step" for applying any useful facets from the past that may actually provide workable effective steps toward true spiritual evolution beyond the currently existent standard issue *"homo sapien"* Human Condition.

Several developments have occurred to assist in moving Seekers through Grades of material concisely. As of March 2020, *Grade-I "Route of Druidism"* was issued in a single master edition volume: MERLYN'S COMPLETE BOOK OF DRUIDISM in addition to the entire *Grade-II "Route of Mesopotamia"* now available in master edition as: NECRONOMICON: THE COMPLETE ANUNNAKI LEGACY.

In this same tradition of mega-anthology textbooks, a complete *Grade-III* omnibus of the *"Route to Mardukite Systemology"* is now collected as SYSTEMOLOGY HANDBOOK, which provides a full sequence of study as follows:

1. MARDUKITE ZUISM (*"A Brief Introduction"*)
2. THE TABLETS OF DESTINY (*"Liber-1"*)
3. CRYSTAL CLEAR (*"Liber-2B"*
4. SYSTEMOLOGY (*"The Original Thesis"*)
5. MASTER COURSE (*"Grade-III Supplement"*)

—additionally including: THE POWER OF ZU

There are many common points that bridge the various Grades and Routes. Most of which become apparent by personal discovery through the *Route of Druidism* and other entry-level perceptions of "New Age" magickal revival, many stemming from beyond even Europe, which is explored within *Grade-II* materials pertaining to Mesopotamia, Babylon and Anunnaki. This bridges directly to the content that inspired THE TABLETS OF DESTINY and the remaining work of *Grade-III*.

: LECTURE 36—THE TABLETS OF DESTINY :
(September 28, 2020)

The Mardukite Master Course is so defined because of a "Master" level of understanding that is applied to what we consider the Master Grades—*Grade-I*, *Grade-II* and *Grade-III*. And so, the Master Course—in Grade-I, we had two textbooks that, basically were meant to establish, and *flatten*, all of the mystery surrounding "magick and mysticism" and "Druidism" and all of the "enchantments" and the "Faerie World" and the "Dragon Legacy" and all of that; and they kind of go together to solidify the *foundation* of what Grade-I material and Grade-I understanding *is*.

And in Grade-II, we are treating, of course, the "Mesopotamian Paradigm"; we're treating the application of cuneiform tablets and the pantheon of the Anunnaki as was understood within the Mardukite Babylonian Tradition—and it is from this that we ended up discovering many of the elements of what we were after to achieve a *higher* point of realization and break forth into that *Third Veil*—that *Third Gateway*—of *Understanding* and *Knowing*.

That it was actually already *right there* within the "Arcane Tablets," so long as an individual was, basically, empowered—or given the ability, or the illumination—to identify these points and to actually see where this was going; to be able to go back and not just do a "reconstruction" of, you know, the "Ancient Mesopotamian" or "Mardukite" tradition as it was observed in ancient Babylon—and not simply do some revival of some 4,000 or plus year tradition; but to take an actual Self-Honest look at what they were doing and what has unfolded since then, and the "Big Picture" of Grade-I and Grade-II and perhaps even where they had come from—but that information had been lost along the way and then reduced to this, kind of, symbolic religio-spiritual mystical methodology.

So, just as the textbooks—"*The Great Magickal Arcanum*" and "*Merlyn's Complete Book of Druidism*"—really go together to form that complete foundation, the establishment of all of our future work: the work beyond Grade-III—the work from the Mardukite Academy and the Systemology Society and beyond—is really built upon the next two tiers on this *Pathway* and that's a combination of Grade-II and Grade-III work; because the overlapping understanding there being, again, ancient Mesopotamia and these Arcane Tablets.

And so, although it wasn't released as such—within the Mardukite Core period—luckily in developing the full Mardukite Master Course, "*Mardukite Zuism: A Brief Introduction*"—this was a booklet that Kyra Kaos and I had established when we were going to structure and formulate the "Mardukite Zuism" path as an extension of where things had come with our Mardukite work as the Chamberlains, and at the same time establishing Systemology.

That is—we discussed that information and *that* is actually a part of "*Necronomicon: The Complete Anunnaki Legacy*"—that is a part of its introduction; we discussed that *last week* in one of those lectures. And in essence, although it was essentially the *last thing* to be included for Grade-III—it's actually *also* included in the Master Edition of the Grade-III textbook, which is "*Systemology Handbook*," and that includes all of the material up until the most recent work—I mean, we're talking within the last few months "work"—all of that material that was developed in the last decade for the field of Systemology.

Now, in addition to "*Mardukite Zuism: A Brief Introduction*," which is how "*The Systemology Handbook*" is actually introduced, because it was established along with, again, "Mardukite Zuism"—the work concerning Systemology as it applies to Mardukite Zuism, when we're talking about the advanced counseling, "processes" and "ministerial work," is basically geared towards two publications: *"The Tablets of Destiny"* and *"Crystal Clear"*—those are the two publications from *The Joshua Free Imprint* that appear as stand-alone (titles), but of which also (are) compiled in *"The Systemology Handbook."*

And this *"Systemology Handbook"* Master Edition—again, this is another "beefy" textbook that includes *literally* all of the work and all of the development and background work going back almost a decade now *of* the modern Systemology Society.

So, for the purposes of our Mardukite Master Course, we're of course going to go through everything that entails, because this is the Master Edition—but, in regards to Mardukite Zuism, the main elements are *"The Tablets of Destiny"* and *"Crystal Clear."* And other than *"Mardukite Zuism: A Brief Introduction,"* as a booklet, you know, so it could be easily distributed, the point of transition between (Grade-II) and Grade-III is *"The Tablets of Destiny"* (the publication).

This is, essentially, an access point that anyone that's been working through this can use, but if you even want to give it to your Seekers as even a Grade-II "graduation-completion" *gift* or something of that nature—*"The Tablets of Destiny,"* although it is not the *first* publication or the *first* work on "Systemology" ever developed, all of the other (previous) work was first developed underground.

A little over—about a year ago, I guess it is—*"The Tablets of Destiny"* was released and its designation is *"Liber-One."* And the idea there being, originally, all of the specific "Mardukite Chamberlain Grade-II Type" Mesopotamian materials for the Mardukite Core—or, you know, the [Complete] *"Anunnaki Bible"*—were intended as having "letter designations," such as *"Liber-N"* for the *"Necronomicon"* or *"Necronomicon Liturgy and Lore"* we had *"Liber-L."* Kind of like what I was mentioning before, with *"Liber-9"*—because, *"Liber-9"* was meant to include more than the three or four "Tablet" series that was included in the [*Complete*] "*Anunnaki Bible*"—it was actually intended to include the material from "*Necronomicon Revelations,*" what was eventually released later as "*Liber-R.*"

But the original designation of "*Liber-9*" [with the intention that it would have included "*Liber-R*"]—the original idea was that the "Systemology" publications, and in that case, a "crossover" or "gateway to the other side"; or "crossover" being "*Liber-9*"—that *all* of our "Systemology" publications would have "numeric" designations to, kind of, differentiate them.

For example, with "*Arcanum*" we have "*Liber-A.*" And even the "Vampire" work—"*The Vampyre's Handbook*" as "*Liber-V.*" Any of the work that was specifically going to be Systemology—which "*Necronomicon Revelations*" is: part describing "esoteric grimoires" and part describing *our* "Systemology"—they were going to have numeric designations.

So, "*Liber-One*" is "*The Tablets of Destiny*" and "*Crystal Clear*" (we discussed briefly the existence of that there) it's "*Liber-2B*"—as in "*to be or not to be.*" So, "*Liber-2B*" is "*Crystal Clear*" and the text for both of those appear in your Grade-III textbook, there, the Master Edition hardcover 2020 "*Systemology Handbook.*"

I want to talk about then—we're going to get into Grade-III or transition to Grade-III using "*The Tablets of Destiny*" text; because, if you've been following along—and *most of the individuals here*, I mean this has become... you've probably read this book several times now—but...

An individual following along, or a Seeker being brought through the Mardukite Master Course sequence of material —the way that I've delivered it—the type of material that we're dealing with in Systemology, which is actually quite advanced and far reaching, in comparison, for example, to the first steps of "ritual magic" and so forth; if you've been following along the progressive *Path* that I've laid out here, the gradients are such a *smooth progression* that *this is* the next logical step, and what's presented here is not going to seem like a "foreign language." It begins right *in* the heart of Mesopotamia.

Now, in regards to archaeology and in regards to historical documents or historical artifacts or museum-quality type of material that scholars and academicians are going to explore, "The Tablets of Destiny" are for all intents and purposes, in regards to Anunnaki mythology, it's really—I mean, we might as well just call this the "Necronomicon." But, without employing "Lovecraftian" overtones.

"The Tablets of Destiny" are this, you know, hugely *enigmatic* powerful facet of the ancient Sumerian tradition and they appear in Babylonian literature. These have *yet* to be actually brought forth, so what we have done—as far as the Systemology Society—is go in an uncover what the *actual*... well, there is: the *"systemology"* of what this actually represents; and that became the basis of what is now the Grade-III (Mardukite) Systemology work.

This concept of the "Tablets of Destiny," if you remember, is introduced in the *Enuma Eliš*—in the "Epic of Creation" and complete backbone of Mardukite Babylonia; and it's these Tablets of Destiny that essentially represent the *Power*, the *Order*, the *Law*—of Tiamat, which she then distributes to Kingu, which Marduk is then able to take, and then using that, becomes the "New Order"—the new "figure" that is, basically, putting the "Cosmos" into *shape*; dividing the "Spiritual" from the "Physical" and the fragmentation of the "Universe" and all that.

It's demonstrating—the story—this isn't to say that Marduk is necessarily the "one" responsible for all of that, but in the Mardukite Tradition, Marduk *is* the "One" who *knows* this knowledge, who *knows* the Way—and basically "beheld" the "Tablets of Destiny" and put things into the Order that they are, and thus understands—understands how *we* got *here*; understands how *we* get *back.*

The "Tablets of Destiny" are meant to distinguish a "Cosmic Law" or "Divine Law" that *orders* the *systems* of, for example, what we consider "Universes." Whereas another type of "Tablet of Destiny" or "Tablets of Fate" in cuneiform literature, and they represent something more akin to what we might consider the "Book of Life"—where an individual's name is inscribed in there, and all of their deeds are recorded and so forth; which is actually what we're dealing with when we're dealing with "imprinting" and "fragmentation" and so forth; what's being carried along with us and which actually shapes our "personality" and shapes our "actions," and beliefs and knowledge; which of course, further shapes our considerations until we've, of course, come down to this Human Condition as we have it.

And then this of course brings up the idea, for example, as "records"—being the idea that a "Book of Life" are *records* of all that was and is and such; the formation of systems, this calls into mind, for example, from other Grades or other traditions, the idea of "Akashic Records"—this "timeline" or "time-track" of which all of existence is, kind of, *moved* through and along with it, the considerations of—well, for example, *of Self*, as it's experienced each of these *variations.*

And, of course, we know that these "Levels" and "Veils" are *alluded* to in other esoteric symbolism—such as the "Kabbalah" and the "Gates" and so forth—and that they represent, essentially, the "divisions" of what is composing the Human Condition.

So, by the time we get into "Systemology," we're dealing a lot with *semantics*, vocabulary—the actual meaning behind things—because it becomes *that much* more critical. That's another one of the "keys" that you can actually take out of Grade-II, when it comes to cuneiform literature; the actual systematization of knowledge and knowing and experience and thinking, in terms of "words" and "vocabulary" and that "shift" in consciousness. That's one of the revelations out of Grade-II material.

And so, in the "Introduction" to, for example, "*The Tablets of Destiny*" or as it appears in the complete Grade-III textbook —"*The Systemology Handbook*"—we discuss the actual cuneiform tablets, we discuss the "Tablets of Destiny" and history very briefly in the "Introduction" to *introduce* the framework of what we're going to be handling.

For example, the word for "*fate*" is NAM; and then for "*destiny*" is NAM-TAR, and that means to "*cut fate*" or to *cut* NAM—so NAM-TAR—or to "ordain" or "decree." And so, when you think about this, it's very interesting—and I've pointed this out long before we even established a text called "*The Tablets of Destiny*," though I forget exactly where.

But, it is very interesting to me, when it comes to "*destiny*" and "*fate*"—these two concepts—that the cuneiform language, as it was written, would actually *differentiate* these two. I mean, we're talking about a language where the word for "eye"— for example, with the IGIGI "*Watchers*"—the word for "*eye*," the word for "*see*" and the word for "*watch*" and all that, was all the same word; whereas obviously there is meant to be a distinction between the words "*fate*" and "*destiny*" and such, as what we consider a "primitive language," would even distinguish the word-signs of these two concepts.

The way I've been explaining it—since the very first "Mardukite Systemology" courses, going back to, I believe, either late 2008 or early 2009, when I was setting down the "*Reality Engineering*" lectures for the first time—*Destiny*, just by, you know, we deal a lot with semantics and word origins in our intellectual study (keep in mind that we're maintaining a literary tradition almost in honor of the scribe-priests of Borsippa within the domain of Babylon)—when we're dealing with the idea of *Destiny*, it should be almost apparent, given the root word there, that we're talking about a "*destination*."

We're talking about the point *to* which a particular course is being traveled; and the *Destination* is a "fixed" point. Now, the way that you might *go to arrive* at that, that's another story, that might be multiple (possible) routes, and that is what we generally refer to as "*fate*," which has more to do with the *nature* of the *Pathway* on which you're traveling or, for example, the Game—the Game of Life.

Fate is *ruled* by *Destiny*, because "*Destiny*" is the firm, standard, fixed—the "ends" so to speak, or the "definitions" of the Game; whereas an individual's "*Fate*" is mainly determined by their own inclinations, their own choices and decisions *within* the confines of the *greater* Game.

It's really this point, when we're talking about "Destiny" and we're talking about the "Tablets of Destiny," we're talking about the *End Goals*; we're talking about the *Pathway* that leads to *Infinity*; we're talking, essentially, that which is *what* the *Ordering* of the *Cosmos* is structured around and those systems.

We're not dealing necessarily in "absolutes"; but we're dealing closely in *that* direction; whereas "*fate*" is really a matter of an individual's experience—it's really, when it comes to the Human Condition, of course that experience, the freedom of choice, is really based on an individual's ability to be *free* of all the imprinting and response-mechanisms that are fixed upon them [or that *they* are fixed upon].

But, this difference between *Destiny* and *Fate* is how "*The Tablets of Destiny*" material is introduced. It's basically introduced with a language lesson by one of our Staff Writers that deals with the Mesopotamian aspects of Systemology—Reed Penn.

It's important for me to illustrate that as we get into this, because there is a distinct *connection* between the cuneiform language and Mesopotamia *and our* presentation of the "Tablets of Destiny" as being a launch point from out of this, you know, "archaic tradition" that has already been so obscure that we dedicate an entire textbook—an entire grade—to the "Route of Mesopotamia" and then *from this* we are pulling out elements to illustrate a higher level of understanding of which you can then, of course, go back and review and find elements of all this.

But, we're talking about *here*, just a very basic—the significance behind this, more than just trying to define terms for an individual about, "Oh what is *destiny*? What is *fate?*"—we've reached a point where there really are no arbitraries in this respect. I'm communicating to you in a spoken language that is represented in a particular culture, which is English, and it's written down—or it's gonna be transcribed in a specific way, which is English.

These particular words are meant to duplicate an understanding that I am trying to communicate *by* delivering these messages; and the meanings behind them, once it gets into the "other end"—once it's reached the receiver—we're dealing with, essentially, a whole different reality; we're dealing with an individual's... we're dealing with *you* and *you...* and *you... all your* "personal universes" as this is being received—and whether or not it's actually one-to-one with what I'm projecting is another story. [*Laughs*]

But, *this* is the first lesson in that—in the very "Introduction" of "*The Tablets of Destiny*" we're differentiating a distinction between *Destiny* and *Fate*; and an individual that, for example, with this basic, you know, semantic lesson is already stumbling over that—this type of... the ability to differentiate, the ability to understand the meanings intended behind one word or another—this is very critical for a Master-Level understanding of Systemology.

Even at a Grade-III level—we're not even, at this point, gonna be dealing with any *upper-level* Grades, or the... anything specific for "Mardukite Ministers" that is not already reflected in *this* textbook—anything regarding "Piloting"—I just plan on taking the rest of the Mardukite Master Course to deliver the Grade-III Mardukite Systemology *as it's* presented in the books—in the textbooks—and how you might treat it in "courses" in your Academies, or when working with your Seekers, regarding the application of this material at a personal level, while still regarding it at an "academic-school" level.

The point when we break here (is) between the Systemology presented in the Mardukite Master Course and the Systemology that we deal with at higher levels or other forms of training—such as the Flight School, which is geared towards Piloting. And "Piloting" is a specific application of the principles that we're going to be spending *the next couple days* covering.

I'm not holding anything back from what's relayed in the material—but, before an individual attempts to *apply* this to "Piloting" and actual "processing" and "spiritual advisement" aside from simply having a Master-Level understanding of this material as an instruction, as a background to "Mardukite Systemology." We want to focus them on *this* mastery first, before trying to take this to that practical level.

And an individual should be able to work *through* this textbook—*"The Systemology Handbook"*—and be able to understand it and apply it to themselves and be able to instruct others in the material specifically that this covers, within the domain of the Mardukite Master Course and the first three "Grades" of the Mardukite Academy of Systemology.

"Piloting" however, is a completely separate aspect—as is what we'll be treating as "Mardukite Zuism" and the "ministry" and "religious" aspects of that as a completely separate aspect of this—(we're focusing) simply (on) the treatment *of this* Grade-III "Mardukite Systemology" material as *information*; as *knowledge*.

A lot of time is spent in *"Tablets of Destiny"*—in that textbook, and of course, within the entire Master Edition of it as well, *"The Systemology Handbook"*—but, as *"Liber-One"* and as the main bridge between what we we're treating as the "Route of Mesopotamia" and the Mardukite Chamberlains and the development of the Mardukite Organization over a decade *and* the Grade-III work of Mardukite Systemology and the Systemology Society and the evolution of Mardukite Zuism, we're treating *semantics* a lot—we're treating the definitions, defining the concepts, making sure that before we start piercing these *higher* levels of understanding, even within the Grade-III work, that we are making sure an individual doesn't go past a point that they don't understand.

This a key point of delivering the Mardukite Master Course at *any* Grade, when you're handling Seekers or when you're representing it—to make sure that an individual isn't moving past a point they don't understand; because, although it may continue to be quite interesting—although they may continue to read or continue to attempt to apply the attention, as much as they can will—the actual *Awareness* begins to dim, because they've already missed something and they're just moving past and going through the motions of reading words, but not actually comprehending and not actually carrying within them what they had achieved up until that point. Honestly, it just kinda gets left off right there, and until an individual goes back and picks it up and goes through whatever it is that they misunderstood, there's no further realizations that are going to be achieved from that, in which to base another level or gradient of understanding.

So keep in mind, I mean, really at the first levels, you know, the primary elements of Systemology—especially at a Grade-III level within the Mardukite Master Course—we're still in the domain of Mesopotamia, but we're treating it a little bit differently; and as we go along, we're *defining* things... Including, for example, when we talk about the Mardukite Paradigm: the idea that a *paradigm* is simply an "all-encompassing standard in which to view the world; a worldview" and then also to communicate reality—it's something you use to represent objects, it's something used to associate other knowledge with; and then others that are in a shared reality, to be able to communicate that same thing. That's what a *paradigm* is.

So, when we're talking about the "Mardukite Paradigm," we're talking about the idea of going back 4,000 years from the Mesopotamian worldview—the view in which to experience the world—and looking at the *Enuma Eliš*, the Epic of Creation, the idea of the "Ordering of the Cosmos"; all of that takes place from the "Infinity of Nothingness" and everything that we've covered in Grade-II, but now in this *new* elevation of the same Mardukite Core, we're going back and actually making certain that we can establish a higher level of understanding from this.

And so, this even goes into making certain that we're *defining* things—and especially those that are being introduced to this for the first time. Because it's not automatically expected that all individuals coming into the Academy or taking courses—I mean, unless you have prerequisites for this—or those that discover the books, since they are available... I mean, you can get these wherever books are sold—that an individual is going to have the background that we've established through the *last week and a half* of the Mardukite Master Course.

It's really up to your abilities as Master-Level Instructors to be able to gauge that and work that out with your own applications; because, you know, if we were just to make it where every individual *had to* go through "ritual magic school" in order to become a "Mardukite Zuist" or *every* individual had to go through the studies of "Mesopotamia" and choose "Mardukite Zuism" in order to get benefit from "systemological processing," well, I mean, that would be ridiculous. Now, it's a little bit different here [*laughs*] when we're talking about the Mardukite Master Course, because this particular course—the appendices of these Master Editions; the fact that we've collected all this stuff together as "Master-Level Grades" and are delivering an "Instructor's Manual" to you and eventually transcripts of this overview of understanding that hasn't necessarily been laid directly *in* the former texts—that's a little bit different.

We're treating *this* Master Course as, basically, an Instructor's Level of education to be able to go and administer "education" and "assistance" in these types of traditions and this kind of work and with Seekers and even establish branches of the Mardukite Academy or the Systemology Society on your own—and be able to actually do that effectively and with access to the same work, you know, these same editions that we use at the Library at the Academy; with access to, for example, these lectures, the information that I can best easily give directly, knowing that an individual already has access to these other materials and is already working at it as an encompassing whole, as opposed to the individual parts or routes.

This is what is making the Mardukite Master Course essentially the upper-most epitome of what we've been able to develop—of what *I've* been able to develop, actually—in twenty-five years of working at this special education for Instructors or a Master-Level education for Seekers that, you know, wished to work through all this on their own—which is also perfectly fine, as long as you have the dedication and fortitude to push through all of these points and get through the bulk of material unaided by any direct assistance. Even the formation of "study groups"—where everyone is working individually, but then also together from the same bodies of material and the same outlines—can be incredibly beneficial in working through this material.

We mentioned a bit about, for example, the Necronomicon; we mentioned a bit about the way that Babylonian magic even developed into the "Kabbalah"; and the "Kabbalah" (even) developed into other traditions of "magic" and "grimoires" and so forth—so, even within, when we're dealing with the cuneiform tablets or the "Arcane Tablets" as the apply to Systemology, we're always dealing with the same "objective reality"—we're dealing with the same *things* "out there," we're dealing with the same "tablets."

We're dealing with the same pieces of material—the difference being our *"level of understanding."* And we kinda throw this around a lot—I mention it a lot fluidly in the vocabulary of the Mardukite Master Course—and usually this is related in connection to the "Gates" and to the *Three Grades* of the Mardukite Master Course as we've relayed it.

So, for example, at our *first level of understanding*, whether we're dealing with cuneiform tablets—such as the *Enuma Eliš*—or we're dealing with any other kind of practices or traditions, we're mainly dealing with "surface magic"; we're dealing with that Grade-I level of understanding that—even if it isn't Grade-I; it could even be Grade-0 [*zero*] for that matter—it could be just *whatever* the "exoteric," you know, the "common denominator"—just the base level understanding that the average member of the population would carry.

And, I mean, this can include all manner of using "prayers" and "devotion" and treating the Anunnaki as "deities" and "idols" and so forth; and it also tends to lead to a lot of "cultural superstition" [also indicative of the early *lunar-cults* of Sumer], which tends to, kind of, overshadow any of the truer elements that may be actually hidden within a particular application of cultural mythology or some kind of practices.

So, that's the *"exoteric"* understanding. And then the *"esoteric"* understanding—when we approach the *second level of understanding*—we're talking about, for example, Grade-II; we're talking about the *systematization* of an *understanding*, for example, as represented by the god Nabu, the Anunnaki deity that's considered the Speaker or the Prophet; the one that's the heir or herald of the Mardukite Tradition and establishing a standard in Babylon in honor *of* his father Marduk.

And this is all done, of course, as the son of the essential hero *of* the *Enuma Eliš* and the representation thereof—this idea of representing in the priesthood and whatnot; but we're talking about the *esoteric* way in which those that were the learned—for example, with the written word and the Hermetic philosophies, and for example, the way in which we've treated the information of ancient Mesopotamia *directly as* "The Route of Mesopotamia."

Once we've, kind of, gotten an individual through the whole "Mystery" of the "magic" and "enchantments" at the Grade-I (level), we don't necessarily have to treat Mesopotamia at that level; and so, in the Grade-II work and the Mardukite Core, we were really treating it as a literary tradition and an intellectual tradition in a way in which individuals were able to elevate their Awareness and their experience and their view of the world—and their relationship with that—by simply having a *higher* understanding at an intellectual level, in terms of language, being able to set down the vocabulary, the semantics.

And so, what this inevitably leads to is, now that we've gone through all that—and all the material from, for example, "*Necronomicon: The Complete Anunnaki Legacy*"—we've, more or less, established and *flattened* the nature and function *of* that "Mystery School" as well.

What we're left with is, basically, anything that we can take from it that's not specific to any of the cultural paradigms—or any specific religious dedication and so forth—but to look at, beyond that, what the Priests were actually knowing and what the Priesthoods were actually after, which is a higher spiritual understanding and organization and systematization of knowledge and (its) application, than what was readily available; either *verbatim* within the literary tradition at Grade-II, or within even the *common* understanding of "magic" and "mysticism."

So, we're dealing with the *secrets*—at Grade-III we're dealing with upper-level secrets of, essentially, any and all of these "Ancient Mystery Schools," "Secret Societies," traditions, cabals, you know, fraternities and so forth; because this is what they've all been leaning towards or seeking to access as a point *beyond* "physical existence." Of course, many of them have not—well, nearly all of them at this point; we don't know of any that have actually pierced these veils up until the work that we've been recently doing—and we've been doing it, leaning on the shoulders of 6,000 of evolution of human civilization of efforts and attempts in this direction; so, it isn't as if we are spawning this from nothing. Okay? But we are already working at—and have already taken—a Master-Level examination of everything that has come before; and after being able to do that, well, *what's keeping us from going forward?*

: LECTURE 37—MARDUKITE SYSTEMOLOGY :
(September 28, 2020)

[*This is the thirty-seventh lecture of the Mardukite Master Course and prior to the break—the early half of the day—we were making our transition from Grade-II into Grade-III; and we just defined what the actual "Three Levels of Understanding" that we've "graded" this on, in relation to the knowledge tiers of the Mardukite Academy Grades and also the Grades as they apply to the Gates.*]

And so, just as I warned you, the graduation of the gradiation [*gradients*] between Grade-II and Grade-III isn't as stark as, for example, when we completed Grade-I and pretty much "called it a day" as a "Magic School." But we are, at this juncture, fully immersed in knowledge lectures specific to the Grade-III material, which was originally classified as the "Master Level" material. We now consider the entire—the Master Grades—as all of I, II and III; but the defining caliber of knowledge and work that went in to finally setting forth the "Mardukite Master Course" is essentially Grade-III.

So, we are now officially in Grade-III—although we are *still* dealing with elements of Mesopotamia, in terms of the presentation of the first work, "*Liber-One*," for Mardukite Systemology, which is "*The Tablets of Destiny: Using Ancient Wisdom to Unlock Human Potential*"—and this material is, of course, found in your Grade-III Master Edition textbook, the hardcover 2020 edition of "*The Systemology Handbook.*"

In other traditions and other esoteric schools, we find the "Ancient Mystery Tradition" essentially fragmented to the same extent that its founders, or those that are delivering the information—the Instructors—are fragmented. For example, there's really no *logical* reason why it should have taken *us*—taken the Mardukite Academy and the evolution of the work of the Mardukite Chamberlains and even my own *twenty-five* year investigation into basically arriving at the work of Mardukite Systemology.

And then, even then, what is that?—*one hundred and fifty years* into the "magical revival" that's been taking place—there's no reason it should have taken this long; but unfortunately, all of the previous "esoteric treatments" of knowledge and the handling of the "Ancient Mystery School" and all of the facets that we kind of blow through in the Mardukite Master Course, and in the textbooks, were essentially treated in *exclusion* and fragmented from one another.

And so, as long as knowledge was treated in fragmentation —as long as the individual's associative knowledge and ability to understand their view of the world and interact with it was all based on fragmented knowledge—then there was no greater achievement with that knowledge could be had. I mean, their just upgrading preexisting conditions and just, kind of, reinforcing them, validating them—basically just trying to make a better "Human being" as the shell that it is, instead of seeking more "metahuman" *higher* pursuits beyond the assumption of it being a "reactive-control mechanism."

In mentioning this—the word "fragmentation" is thrown around a lot in the Mardukite Master Course. It's introduced, really, at the early grades of material, in regards to knowledge or in regards to an individual and their state. And what it really means is "a fractioning of the wholeness" or a "fracture" of this "holistic, interconnected" *Alpha* state —a primary or prime state—which is then essentially "fractured."

Kind of like if you were to take a *crystal* and 'smack' it—you would end up with all of these broken lines and stuff through it; you may not break it, but all of a sudden it's not going to *reflect* or *refract* the same quality of light. In essence, that's what happens [*laughs*] to an individual as they take on more and more *considerations* that are inaccurate.

For example, inaccurate knowledge associations or reactive-emotional conditioning concerning various *facets* of Life; their abilities; their personal *willingness* to *reach* towards new things or (if) they 'shudder' away from certain things—all that can be programmed and all of that is part of what we treat as "fragmentation."

The opposite of that is a term that we use, pretty much, since 2009 or 2008 is when I first started introducing it—and it actually appears in the "introductory" sections of the original presentation of our *"Necronomicon"* or our [*Complete*] *"Anunnaki Bible"*—but it's a concept called *"Self-Honesty."* And "Self-Honest Clarity" is like, for example, having a "clear crystal"—one that is not fragmented; one that can shine through: the same image that is put forth to it is the same that it's projecting.

It's a *one*-to-*one duplication*. As opposed to, for example, a "function-machine." A function-machine would be, for example, if you were to imagine a metaphoric *box*—and this is how they would teach math when I was elementary school for different equations—for example, you know, if "*x*" is *three*, or we put a "3" in a *box*, every time we enter something into the box, it's going to "*add 3*" to it—you know, you could have a *seven* in front of it, and you put the "7" *into* this function-machine and it *adds-3* and the result is a "10."

What happens with an individual is they *have* "function-machines" that are basically "functioning" with these various *programs*, *imprints* and all types of mechanism where, depending on what is called up—now it may not always be the same function. They may have certain different functions attached to certain different encounters, so that they've been programmed that, well, "every time you encounter an individual that has *long black hair*, because of this *other* encounter and the *associations* with it, you will then pull up this other information and process your *reality* based on that predisposed function."

And so, that's basically—that's what "fragmentation" is: *not* to have a *one-to-one* understanding or experience with reality. And most individuals carrying the Human Condition, that have found themselves in low-states of consideration or that they've been trapped—their point of view has been entrapped—they believed, you know, conditioned themselves and then forgotten any higher state and believe themselves entrapped in and only *as* the Human Condition; those people are very much "fragmented."

The idea that we can do a *reversal* of this—and the idea of *defragmentation*—is, of course, the pinnacle of the work of "Systemology Processing." I mean, that's the whole point.

"*Crystal Clear*," the textbook, which is also within your Master Edition textbook—but that was released based on the courses and workshops I was giving like a year ago; a practical guide that would be our "Self-Defragmentation Program." So, it was a way of actually almost "running" an "anti-virus program" or something on the basic condition of the Human being—and kind of cleaning up the "genetic vehicle" and its "Mind-Systems."

And then this leads to—you know, as we go further into Systemology—we deal with more and more "control" and "command" over that Mind-System and its relationship between *Self* and a "genetic vehicle." But, getting an individual *just* to the point of *realizing* these things and even *clear* to a point of what is happening around them, who they are as being a Spiritual Being occupying or *operating* a "genetic vehicle." These are pinnacle points on which—until they're established, one can really go no further.

When we speak of "Self-Honesty," we are talking about the closest one can get, at this juncture at least, from the point we are talking about "beta-defragmentation" in Grade-III—

so, we're talking about a state of *Being* and *Knowing* that is, just, as close to *Alpha* as possible, in a clear and present total Awareness of an as *Self*—the "I-AM"—and that they are free of the artificial attachments, perceptive filters, emotional reactive mental programming; all that's imposed *on* the Human Condition *by* a "systematized" *physical existence*—the "Physical Universe"—the "beta-existence" and its participation.

That's one of the key points in Grade-III. There are *a lot of* points in Grade-III that are fairly critical. It's a little bit more involved in some respects than the others because it's —we're dealing with "ancient concepts," the type of stuff we've been dealing with for the *last couple weeks*, but with a "modern" understanding now, and not just trying to duplicate *them* one-for-one; because they already *aren't*, they've already been fragmented down thousands of years of various cultures and various opinions and various fragmented individuals that set them down.

So, there's really no point in trying to actually duplicate or follow, you know, all of that exactly as it's given—the point being that: as a result of it, coming to us in that respect, some element of these, you know, what we treat at Grade-III, has *survived* within the widespread symbols and aspects and traditions and all the various ways in which it has come to us through 6,000 years of—well, I'd say "development," but *we're* really developing it *now*. We're taking everything from 6,000 years ago, from almost a "Golden Age" and watching its degradation into everything up unto the modern "magical revival" and then we're taking it to the next step with Grade-III.

Mardukite Systemology—it is referred to as "Mardukite" Systemology, because we are applying it *from* the "Mardukite" tradition; it was the "Mardukite" tradition that basically *sponsored* the Mardukite Academy, and it was the work *of* the Mardukite Chamberlains that, basically, is the reason *why* we even have "Systemology"—but also to make sure that we are *branding* our particular tradition; for example, everything that falls within the domain of the Mardukite Master Course.

Although "Mardukite" being named, of course, for Mesopotamia—and being that the core of where we, kind of, look from in the development of the Master Grades and even my work in the past twenty-five years, up until the newer developments of Systemology—we've been looking out from; rather than looking from the present and looking *back* 6,000 years, we've gone back to the original Mardukite paradigm and then, basically, looked *forward* and seen exactly how things de-evolved and developed into how they are today; but looking at it from its original "pure" perspective.

So, the purposes of modern "Mardukite Systemology" is, again, classifying it as such—which is the technical classification of Grade-III: it would be "The Route of Mardukite Systemology." And that's not to say that it's remaining centric to Mesopotamia, although of course, we're basing it off the "Tablets of Destiny" and progressing and transitioning from Grade-II to Grade-III using that as a bridge.

But, the idea being: that it is *from* the "Mardukite" brand—just as there is "Mardukite Zuism"—and that is to differentiate it from other forms of "Zuism." Then, "Mardukite Systemology" is to differentiate it from other pursuits of any kind of "systematology" or studies of the same and those other applications that one might find out there.

And then of course, the context of this *higher* route of spiritual work and the defragmentation and whatnot being *called* "Systemology," is kind of, you know, so similarly sounding to some *other* organizations—and what that may represent at this juncture—is just one of those unfortunate coincidences that one might end up having to deal with, much like the semantics of the "*Necronomicon.*"

But this background—just as we were able to explain the

context of the *"Necronomicon"*—I think, by the end of the Mardukite Master Course, you will have more than enough within your arsenal to be able to even explain the entire functional purpose behind us calling it "Systemology."

Systemology, of course, is named for the entire intellectual pursuit and scientific—whether it be physical or spiritual—regarding the structure of *systems*. And when we're talking about *systems*, especially at an *esoteric* level, the highest pinnacles of that being, as we've covered it in the Mardukite Master Course: we have the Druids, which are the *great systematizers* in the European lands, and then we have Babylon, which predated that, but was the great origin of the systematization which it did in its own world in its own right.

So what we've been dealing with Systemology, systematization, the idea of systems, one thing affecting another thing —you know, this whole concept—we've been dealing with this since the very beginning. The only difference is that now, at the Master-Level, we've been able to actually call it —you know, we say we're calling it: "*is* what it *is*"—we're basically *is*-ing it; and having a certain higher level of understanding just as a result of that; by taking out the "Mystery" or taking out all the other perceptions and filters that might get in the way of actually seeing things for what they *are*.

At this transition point, we've just approached it, for example, from the context of the *legendary* "Tablets of Destiny"—which, of course, represent this idea of "Divine Truth" and the "Supreme Knowledge" and this "Cosmic Power" of the "gods" as they're represented as the "Anunnaki."

And this is first, for example, introduced in—for these purposes—in ancient Mesopotamia. This is the point when we see the Anunnaki figures, we see the integration of the *Enuma Eliš* or the "Tablets of Creation" to basically represent the "Mardukite" paradigm. And we see the "sealing" of this with like a "higher class," which is at first essentially the Anunnaki as being almost a separate "Star Race" or "inter-dimensional race" or some kind of remainder from another civilization, again, *prior* to the inception of the *one* that *we're* in the shadows of *now*.

And this is all brought together within that idea of a "priesthood" and that literary level [*legacy*]—and then, of course, we're looking at this higher level of knowledge; we're moving beyond any of the *exoteric*, the *outer* perceived concepts of traditions, the *outer* shells of these "planetary pantheons" and "gods" and "goddesses" and all of these various traditions that have spawned from that. We've already explored that, we've looked at that—we've seen what it does. We have now thousands of pages of material to support a Research Library regarding that.

We're looking to deeper *esoteric* levels, such as was understood by the priests—and maybe not even actualized within their own "wisdom philosophies," because we really can't be certain what an individual, on their own, what kind of outcome or consequences of any of these spiritual applications that they've had. But, that is the direction in which we are working.

So, we've been able to find, again, the "Three Levels" with the physical understanding being transferred to a more intellectual wisdom-philosophy or Hermetic understanding, and then of course, trying to use that to free ourselves from the gravity of this low-level physical existence *into* reaching new levels of advancement—of Awareness and Actualization as *Self* as Spirit, as the Alpha-Spirit, the Prime Spirit of Self *before* all of this fragmentation: which is the Pathway to Self-Honesty.

We've talked a bit—because it's virtually impossible to even cover the Tablets of Destiny without covering the *Enuma Eliš*. So we've crossed this ground already, in many ways, when we are studying the Grade-II material concerning the exploration of the "Epic of Creation" as it was used for ordering the Babylonian Mardukite systems and paradigm of: Marduk *using* the Tablets of Destiny in order to basically achieve Self-Honesty *on his own*, and with that, "Divine Knowledge" and then governing the "Cosmic Ordering."

And it is from there that we begin to define, for example, the division of systems between the "Spiritual Universe" and the "Physical Universe" or "Alpha" and "Beta" existences; and those concepts are what distinguish Mardukite Systemology because we starting to use this higher level of semantic understanding—this higher level of vocabulary—which wasn't necessarily as present *in* Grade-II.

We integrated "Mardukite Zuism" [with Grade-II] because now at the Master-Level we've been able to work far enough beyond strictly what was considered the "Mardukite Core" to now include the concept of "Mardukite Zuism" as a tradition and its systemology—but, at the time, the idea of... it's only loosely associated about the idea between the "physical" and "spiritual." It's all actually in there; we're just taking it to the next step and we're treating "Alpha-existence" and "Beta-existence" as examples in the direction of "AN" or "KI" (in Mardukite Systemology).

Mardukite Systemology and Mardukite Zuism applies, for example, the concepts such as: *Alpha-Spirit*, which is what we refer to as the "True Self" or "I-AM," the Spirit that is actually controlling the physical body or the "*genetic vehicle.*" And it does so using a "life-line" or this "continuum" of Spiritual "ZU" Energy that we call the "ZU-line."

We referred to the concept of "ZU" already in our Grade-II work, but that—we're dealing with this *spectrum* or this *continuum*, almost like an "Identity Continuum" of Spiritual Life Energy or "ZU" that extends *from*—as an Awareness—the point of the Alpha-Spirit into whatever beta-range of consideration it has, whatever point-of-view it's maintaining within beta-existence.

And "Beta-existence" is, of course, what we're classifying the "Physical Universe" and the direction of "KI"—but the manifestations in the "Physical Universe" that are separate or *interior* to both what you can see around you with the matter and objects *and then* also the "Mind-System" *of* the Human Condition that's attached *to* the reception of, you know, the "parameters"—the "range"—of whatever can be perceived as "Beta-existence" in exclusion to, for example, an "Alpha-existence" or a "Spiritual Existence."

In *"The Tablets of Destiny"* and Mardukite Systemology—the Grade-III work—the individual is introduced to the actual explanation that I started getting into in Grade-II concerning the *Enuma Eliš* and the fragmentation of Tiamat—being the All separating from the "Infinity of Nothingness—representing the "Potential Everythingness," which could then be divided between the "Spiritual Existence" and then a separate "Physical Existence," where there is a barrier or "Gate" that is separating the two.

This is, basically, the backbone of the "Standard Model of Systemology" and although we have taken it to much further extents, in relation to the *seven-plus-one* divisions of the Gates and to various aspects of the Human Condition and even made an alternate version of it concerning "Spheres of Existence" and the manner in which they influence one another and energetically ripple across the ALL.

All of this is actually—and this is why it's considered an *extension* of Mesopotamia or the Mardukite Tradition or why we are considering it Mardukite Systemology; and then of course presenting the introduction of it—the *"Liber-One"* as *"The Tablets of Destiny"*—we're using the *Enuma Eliš* to establish the fundamental framework for the "Standard Model" on which we were able to develop all of the rest of Systemology, and *continue to* to this day.

We're currently working on—*I'm* currently working on wrapping up materials for Grade-IV; I mean, we've already begun various explorations into Grade-V. So, we *do know* that there *is* somewhere to go; that this isn't a dead-end trail—and we're always working a little bit ahead of whatever is being presented [*published*]; *just* to make sure that The Way ahead *is* clear.

The first evolution that we actually had, in regards to the Standard Model, is that we basically had a *direction* of "AN"—which was basically *toward* "Infinity"—and we had a *direction* of "KI"—which is towards the "material continuity" of the "Physical Universe" of "beta-existence." And then the *only* point of impingement—the *only real* point of connectivity—between the two, and we drew a *line* through it, was the "ZU-line"; and the "ZU-line" being the Awareness or the "Life-force" or the actual Spiritual Energy *of* Self, looking *into*, directing its Awareness, its point-of-view, its own "ZU"—its own *Knowingness*—through the various spaces and Universes and everything to reach the point of considerations that it has *here*.

And this was a very basic Model to work from and to develop from, but it—at that point—still heavily based strictly on the development of the *Enuma Eliš* and the progression of the "Tablets of Creation" and how the Universe was formed and fragmented.

Hermetic philosophies and the other attempts to reach Grade-III, have always applied the point of Self—mistaken the point of Self; the Awareness; the one that is actually having the experience—with the Source being the Absolute or the Infinity of Nothingness. They were never able to conceive of the Infinity of Nothingness and would therefore put this center-point in the middle of a circle and say that "that center point was God or was Source and that its echoes or vibrations rippled outward from that epicenter."

And although the context behind that is *kind of* close in some respects, the Model that we have, as far as the Infinity of Nothingness occupying outside of it, and from that upper-most point—the point of Alpha—that it is the individual, their Awareness, that is extending out from beyond that. And that the individual—the actual *Alpha Spirit*—isn't moved; it hasn't changed *its* location. It's the *considerations* of where its surroundings; almost like what you consider "virtual reality" today.

Many of the concepts that are actually behind systemology that we've discovered—that pertain to the highest levels and the direction of "point-of-view," the concept of the "Alpha-Spirit" through multiple "fragmented Universes"—this stuff is starting to actually run *very close* to the kind of, you know, film and "science-fiction" medias and various things that you might see; because the understanding has just been increased, you know?

It would be very difficult to relay the idea of "artificial reality" or a "virtual reality" or various "electronic implants" and stuff to, you know, someone that really has *no* conception or reality on such things—but, in many respects when we look at what's all possible out in existence, we *can't* believe that this is the *first time* that we're coming across these things.

So, really, outside of the realm of the "mystical," the only field that's really ever tried to *tap*—as far as the "sciences" and "philosophies" are concerned; and I don't mean like the philosophies of "epistemology," the study of knowing and knowledge and what is true and such, but—the realm of "*psychology.*" We run up, kind of, against the realm of "psychology" when we approach Systemology; because what we are basically treating at a *spiritual* level—and in "Mardukite Zuism," even at a *religious* level—we're treating the ZU-line as what has been otherwise classified as "consciousness."

And it's been, you know, *long*... the philosopher or the psychologist that's wanted to understand the idea of "consciousness," but since psychology became more of a "behavioral" study, in relation to the Human Condition, and ba sically started treating Humans as *animals*, and *animals* in substitution of Humans and all that—their knowledge base faltered. They weren't able to *tap* anything any higher like we are with our Systemology.

By not even understanding what "consciousness" *is*, I mean... It's really the energetic flow of Awareness. It's a principle system of manifestation; that's Awareness. It's the Awareness that *is* the Observer *actually* there to "witness" and "experience"—or the "*Beingness*" component—that *is* "seeing" or "experiencing" the manifestations that are taking place around.

Before something can be experience, the point of *Beingness* or the Observer must be present for that to take place. This isn't a whole... you know, "if a tree falls in the woods and no one hears it" type stuff—we're not getting into that. We're talking about what *is* "consciousness"; what *is* "Awareness." *Awareness* as a principle of manifestation *is* the Observer that is *aware of* the manifestation.

When we talk about this *Pathway*, or we talk about this *Ladder of Lights*, or we talk about this *ZU-line*, or this point-of-considerations as *Self* that travels through all these different "spheres" between the point of Alpha-Spirit and the physical mundane reality on Earth, we're talking about the esoteric *Pathway to Self-Honesty*.

The Grade-III work is called "Mardukite Systemology" or the "Route of Mardukite Systemology" but, *that's* only the way it is treated within the Mardukite Master Course—as the Master-Grade level of instruction; as *you as* Master-Level Instructors delivering Master-Grades of material. However, in Systemology, the Grade-III work is referred to as "*The Pathway to Self-Honesty.*" That's the premise on which it's launched from.

This is the kind of thing—I mean, if you're looking at any kind of examples in the past, we're talking about, you know, the "Ascended Masters"; those that... they themselves *were* able to achieve these points of higher realization and Self-Honesty even if it wasn't able to be duplicated fully in any surviving literature from them or even the followers that took after them.

When we look at the principles, too, behind for example, the "Tablets of Destiny," the actions of Marduk in regards to the *Enuma Eliš*, we're talking about our ability to Self-Direct and enact a change in [relation] to the environment; and *that's* what we consider "Self-Determinism." And we now realize that "Self-Determinism"—the abilities, the willingness, the reach of Self-Determinism—is actually *proportional to* the level of understanding, the level of responsibility, the level of actual power and control that an individual will be able to wield.

And *this* is what we're able to use as a gradient, so to speak, concerning where an individual *is* on the *Pathway*—and that's up to *them* at this point. In terms of the Mardukite Master Course, we're of course talking about various "Grades" of "material"—we're talking about specific "knowledge grades"—like *these textbooks*, in this case, "*The Systemology Handbook*," which is the Master-level textbook for Grade-III—we're talking about a specific set of information; specific parameters or a specific range of knowledge that each one of these Grades encompasses.

But, from *this point on*, when it comes to, for example, the "Systemology Society," you're talking about a much more subjective experience—you're talking about what the individual is able to experience on their own; you're talking about their own reactivity, their own Pathway, the "*fate*" in which they have taken to *reach* this point and the same Pathway that they're going to take to basically get out—to get through it and get out. And so that becomes a very individualistic thing.

Now, the methodology behind it is set up right here in

Grade-III "Mardukite Systemology" and then is developed further with our "spiritual advisement" and "counseling techniques" that's derived for Mardukite Zuism for the advanced forms of Systemology—or what we consider "piloting." But, for the purposes of the Mardukite Master Course, we're talking about still treating the material at an intellectual level; we're not talking about any particular "mental states" that an individual *has to achieve* to reach these points.

All of them will be "graded" on their own, on a completely different "gradient" versus the kind of "class structure" or "grade structure" that we're dealing with here. The Pathway *still* does follow the "planetary divisions"—we're still following the *Ladder of Lights*, so-to-speak, that we've been describing throughout the Mardukite Master Course—but, by the time that we get to the upper-levels, the Pathway to Self-Honesty, the way its treated in Systemology and the spiritual counseling and so forth, we're not really looking at Seekers as "students" or treating stuff at an academic level; we're actually treating the "practical applications," the "spiritual technologies," the efforts which one can actually demonstrate from this knowledge in a practical sense and working with individuals on that level.

At the point in which we start getting *too far* into that, we'll end up closing off the Mardukite Master Course; because, again, this isn't going to be a replacement for the assistance to educate a "Mardukite Minister" or in terms of the "Flight Schools" for "Pilots" and other "procedures" that are being used. We have a lot of knowledge material, intellectual material and writings within "*The Systemology Handbook*" that have been collected over the last ten years that we use to gain a Master-level understanding of all of this material before forward—and it is at *that* point that we consider an individual having completed the Mardukite Master Course.

: LECTURE 38—GRADE-III DEFINED :
(September 28, 2020)

Where "Mardukite Zuism" kind of *fills a need* or almost replaces the concepts that are prevalent in the modern "New Age" or the revival of, for example, neopaganism and traditions and so forth—it's practical spiritual advancement as "Mardukite Systemology" almost runs parallel with many of the *highest* pursuits of the original intentions behind, for example, psychology and some of the other material sciences that have, unfortunately, degraded and developed to the points that *they* have.

But, being at—we consider it "Systemology"—what we are pertaining this to specifically is the "*holistic*" consideration of *All* existence: of Life, the Universe and Everything—all existences and the *systems* of the same in a "*holistic*" understanding, so that we're not doing the same thing that we've found with all the sciences fragmenting and running in each of their own directions.

Here, we are bringing the pieces back together—bringing and understanding—bringing an interest in having an unified understanding in a way that is being done by, again, *operating* from a *higher* "tier" of understanding; not being down in the "muck" and trying to piece together all these puzzles—*nobody knows what they are* and nobody knows anything about the nature of these puzzles. You've got people running around in every direction wondering what pieces they have and what puzzle they fit to and the number of puzzles that might be in play at this juncture—this all runs pretty much together.

So, when we talk about Mardukite Systemology, we're talking about using a framework that goes back to the original understanding—as we were talking about the early formation of the Standard Model as we were developing it from cuneiform texts, from the Arcane Tablets. This is an understanding that: Okay, maybe, even though it's workable—because we can create this whole paradigm around it—it's the oldest paradigm we have; so if *it* isn't anywhere close to the truth, anything that we consider afterward, any of these other traditions, any of these other cultures that derive their lore from it—that took it and changed it into something else—*what hope do we have* in looking into *those* particular aspects for anything true or to carry us higher?

Really, at the very least—I mean, we're basically going back to the *origins* of everything, to the inception of the systems, the sources behind our experience of the Human Condition *in* modern society; and we're moving from that point. If that's considered wrong—or there's nothing to be had there—then there's no point to anything at all; because this is the logical point in which to work from.

When we talk about our "Standard Model" or the backbone of it—or what defined it—we're using that same representation that we've taken from the *Enuma Eliš*: having an "Infinity of Nothingness" as the background static; and then the existence of which there's the "Everythingness"—The All—that's inherent within the All is the "Tablets of Destiny." Tiamat representing the Law and the All, moving—movement—across the "Oceans" and carrying with (her) the "Tablets of Destiny." The "Tablets of Destiny" representing "Potential Everythingness."

And then, of course, the "control" of this being directed between—you know, we've got the example of this in the *Enuma Eliš* and Marduk taking control of the "Tablet of Destiny" and the "Ordering of the Cosmos." And so, this basic framework is what we use to set our "Standard Model of Systemology" against.

As we can demonstrate—particularly with the Mardukite Master Course; particularly whether you want to go back

6,000 years or look from now backwards 6,000 years—whichever direction you look at it, you can clearly see a *clear* "wisdom tradition" and the "true knowledge" and the *duplication* of the perfect understanding that all of this had originated as—or what's represented as the "Tablets of Destiny" —it obviously is not perfectly communicated down the line. It's basically taken—even myself—it took an extra decade after completing the bulk of the "Mardukite Core" to finally get around to synthesizing just a "perfect understanding" of it.

Prior to the modern inception, in late 2019, of Mardukite Systemology with the publication of "*The Tablets of Destiny*," we had had several different discourses and publications concerning "Systemology" and its developed released to the underground for the last decade, but it wasn't until "*The Tablets of Destiny*" and until we reached a "Master-level" understanding of Grade-II and was able to define it as what our Grade-III work is—for example, what we're dealing with now—that we could go any further.

And it took a considerable amount of time, given not only the "politics" of what was taking place concerning the organization; also, various challenges that I was jumping through in personal life in *just* maintaining a steadfast ongoing full-time pursuit of this work.

There's many allusions that this concept, or this idea, of the "Ancient Mystery School" or the "Tablets of Destiny" or the "Key to the Cosmic Wisdom of the Universe" and all that—has been withheld, or represents the power behind what is *used* to program the masses or fragment the Human Condition away from Self-Honesty, which is mainly geared toward the enforcement and misuse of control in society.

This is the type of information, I mean, you know, when we're dealing with Grade-I, we're dealing with a lot of *outer* level stuff that most individuals—really with a trip to their local bookstore—can pretty much dig up. Not the extent and not necessarily the understanding that we're dealing with; but they're dealing with semantics and concepts that are more readily available. And then when you start to *pierce back* at a little more higher levels of that—well, of course, you've got the whole "Mystery School" and the "Hermetic Orders" and all of that, which pretty much got bungled up in Grade-II—and really never got farther than that.

If there is this more—*higher*—echelon that's been holding onto it, that would be where a lot of the "conspiracy theories," you know—people talk about the Illuminati and all these different "forces" operating, those who are "in the know." That doesn't necessarily mean that this wisdom has given them any greater sense of ethic in terms of their application of "material control" and "operation" of the *systems* that are within their command—or whatever systems they're operating under for that, you know, or are above them.

But it would basically *this* level of "Grade-III Mardukite Systemology" that we would begin to deal with anything that runs parallel with that kind of level—I mean, we've run parallel with virtually everything else that—from the rural Witch's coven to the Hermetic Orders to anything of that nature when we've gone through all the materials of the Mardukite Master Course from Grade-I.

And at *this* point, we're really dealing with the stuff that's really at the upper-most level of what's even been done or delivered in the outer world—or what's even accessible to most people, even if they *do* piece it all together on their own; and it was from *that* systematization that we've been able to base *any* "higher" levels that we consider our "Advanced Systemology."

Unlike Grades I and II, prior to this Mardukite Master Course, we've never had anyone outside of the Academy teaching or instructing any courses on Systemology—so, this is kind of a new terrain, where it comes to some... even if you're familiar with some of the work we've been doing in the last ten years, or twenty-five years, "Mardukite Systemology" and the Systemology paradigm is a very unique evolution of everything that's come before.

And so we haven't... we never really established any set curriculum other than the delivery of the two main texts—"*The Tablets of Destiny*" and "*Crystal Clear*"—both of which appear in "*The Systemology Handbook*" along with a wealth of other material; but the structure of "*The Tablets of Destiny*"— there's chapter summaries at the end of each chapter. There's an outline of them in your "*Instructor's Manual.*"

The other thing that would be of exceptional use is anything dealing with vocabulary or definitions. We spend a lot of time in "*The Tablets of Destiny*" breaking from the instruction to make sure that we've completely defined a new or obscure word; and then, thereafter we start using "footnotes" any time certain words appear. This led to the establishment of a "dictionary"—well, it started as a "glossary."

The "NexGen Systemology Glossary" idea began with "*Reality Engineering*" and when we compiled all the "*Original Thesis*" materials into the "*Awakening*" book—those ones are since out-of-print, but the materials from them have actually been reprinted in "*The Systemology Handbook.*" So, you can still look back to see where things developed from, over the last ten years—and we'll go over some of that here in the Master Course.

But, the outline for "The Tablets of Destiny" and the introduction to Grade-III material, using that as a bridge from Grade-II and coming from Mesopotamia and moving into our Systemology paradigm, is actually also found in that appendix to "*The Systemology Handbook*" and in your "*Instructor's Manual*" and you can use that for a basis—I mean, make sure, if you're going to be establishing any courses— Grade-III Courses—because we haven't really done that or established anything for that before the Master Course.

That was one of the reasons we wanted to *do* the Mardukite Master Course. I had already been treating the "Merlyn School" since the 1990's, and then we had established back in 2010-2011 a certain criteria as a standard in which to certify "Mardukite Ministers" and "Instructors" of the "Mardukite Core" in the underground—but, *this* is the first time we are presenting this new standard.

Of course, *now* we have all these Master Editions, these big hardcover textbooks to represent the four different routes: "*The Great Magickal Arcanum*," "*Merlyn's Complete Book of Druidism*," "*Necronomicon: The Complete Anunnaki Legacy*" and "*The Systemology Handbook*." And in addition to that, we have the appendices from those, that basically have the outline or Instructor's material for the Mardukite Master Course at each Grade; *those* are compiled in the "Instructor's Manual" we have been using here to follow along *loosely* with here [*laughs*], since I've departed from the outline on many points during this Master Course.

[*But we've been actually been able to cover even more ground and even ended up extending the course to include an addition eight lectures, so that we could make certain to have covered each grade fully. And so that outline changed a few times as far as the "Master Course Outline." The "Outlines" in the books are sound as far as the way the materials are presented at each Grade and each Route within the books. And then, of course, we have these actually "Master Course Lectures" that we've been giving—and then eventually a companion to your "Instructor's Manual"—that will include all of the transcripts once we can work all those out properly.*]

This is an incredible wealth of material that—if you're bringing it to an Academy level or you're trying to establish "study groups" or even just working at it on your own—this is a tremendous amount of material that's... I mean, it's taken me a quarter-of-a-century of development; and granted there were many points along the way that I could have actually—I would have been able to get this a little bit *farther* a little bit *faster*...

But, doesn't matter; we're *here now* and that's what's important; we're delivering this now. We're getting it recorded—we're getting it all taped, and so we can make certain now, with the preservation of the materials and me actually taking, well, basically, greater control of the legacy of the material by forming an independent publishing imprint—The Joshua Free Imprint—to make certain that we could maintain total control and distribution power over these materials, and not just be restricted to, like what some of done, in terms of self-publishing or just working through various channels.

We've basically now got the Mardukite Master Course *in the bag*... not to say we're done with the lectures—but we have what we *need* for it *in the bag*. We've got the inception of "Mardukite Zuism" for our *religious* aspects—and then also for the spiritual and philosophical extension of even that, we have our "Systemology" and the "Mardukite Academy" *here*, basically being housed at the "Borsippa Headquarters," which is basically the site of the "Founding Church of Mardukite Zuism" here in Monte Vista, Colorado.

Obviously we're here to stay. We've established a very solid legacy, an incredible Esoteric Library of materials, a whole bunch of very helpful and very actualized staff—and at a distance too—this is, we have... This is not just *here* at the Academy; this is happening all over the world. The point being that: "Mardukite Systemology" is *still* in its development stage.

We've been able to cap off Grade-III and I've been able to revise and formulate an anthology—"*The Systemology Handbook*"—that contains all of the materials, whether it be from "*Tablets of Destiny*" or "*Crystal Clear.*" As I mentioned, it also included the "*Mardukite Zuism: A Brief Introduction,*" which we also bring in to the situation for Grade-II.

We also have "*The Power of Zu*" lectures, which we given a year ago and that was kind of an "open lecture series" that was basic—beginners—anyone and everyone was allowed; it wasn't Systemologists only. And those transcripts now appear in "*The Systemology Handbook*" in addition to the material of "*The Original Thesis*" of Systemology—which included several different booklets that were released in the underground nearly a decade ago. And other highlights from, for example, the "*Reality Engineering*" lecture series from, again, nearly a decade ago.

So, this is basically what "*The Systemology Handbook*" is—is a complete—the research and discovery and development of all the elements that we are now using as a basis for all the "Wizard Grades" and *upper-level* work, and everything that's beyond the Mardukite Master Course—basically is all contained within this handbook. Some of the material is there for posterity; some of the material is there for education; some of the material is there just because it was *already there* and needed to be included to be complete—and make sure we weren't cutting anything out of the books in order to include them (all).

But, as far as an educational level, *this* is the first time I'm actually delivering an overview of "Mardukite Systemology" *ever*. I've delivered various lectures for "*Tablets of Destiny*" when that was being developed; when we were developing the "*Crystal Clear*" Self-Actualization manual and workbook, I delivered several lectures at that time too—and I've done this very pointedly, given various workshops and experiments that were going into the development of various books.

But, *this* Mardukite Master Course is *literally* the *very first* time—unlike me giving the... some of you *here* have even heard me give the "Anunnaki-101" radio interview half a dozen times on various "shows" and "podcasts" in the last decade; or have heard, you know, everything about the "Necronomicon" or actually even have had some of the outlines for this material from our original group-leaders handbook called *"Guardians of the Gates"* that was released almost a decade ago, when we were still working specifically within the Mardukite Chamberlains ("Core").

Unlike all of *that*—and the "YouTube" videos and the various books and the time spent with them—*this* is still pretty "fresh." And I've never really gotten into "Mardukite Systemology" on any of the radio programs; I've dealt with it very minimally, in terms of public broadcast—I've really spent the last year, really, full time in dedicated development of it. So, *here* is the first time that we're actually giving an overview of it; talking about it after the fact, after it was written.

Now, then, when we examine some of this work from "*The Tablets of Destiny*" material, we find a certain sequence of information—the sequence being followed (as) given in the Tablets of Destiny and the Arcane Tablets, the *Enuma Eliš*, the Creation Tablets—all of this being used to formulate, essentially, a workable spiritual philosophy and this begins with the "cosmology" or the "Standard Model of Systemology," which is how we define and order our understanding of *all* existences; *all* Life in *all* existences in *all* Universes between here and Infinity.

This use of ancient wisdom—this is what is actually demonstrated on the "Tablets of Destiny" because, obviously, when we're dealing with the Sixth Gate even, we're dealing with the Realm of Marduk *proper*, we're talking about "Cosmic Ordering" —the "Ordering" of Universes; the "Creation" of Universes; the "Games" of Universes; all of the activity and the motions.

And that's one of the things that we find—especially in *this* "beta-existence"—all things in this Universe are *in* motion. All activity is essentially a motion that these *things*—the objects themselves—and anything else between them, the energy and matter and space, as it's measured across time or distance, it's a *wave-motion*. And so, we're talking about a higher understanding... Really, we're dealing with, essentially, "quantum physics" and "dimensional theory" and all of *that* in Systemology.

Our Systemology is really *not just* the "mystical" and "magical"—or the "occult" and "religious" and "mythological"—understanding that we've worked and walked a Pathway *through* in order to get to *this* point in the Mardukite Master Course; we're actually dealing with—I mean, the essence of, you know, the "fabric" of Space and Time and understanding Energy and Matter and the position of *Self* and *Awareness* and its relationship with all this.

I mean, we're dealing with the *highest* level of understanding that's possible *from* what has been given; what we have found over the last 6,000 years—and of course, this is leading us to our *own* work and the development of *more* than what has been here before. And that is what we refer to as the "Wizard Levels" *beyond* the "Master Levels"—beyond, for example, even *this* Grade-III intellectual understanding of it as "Mardukite Systemology"; we're talking about what is *beyond* the Master Course, about "Wizard Levels."

It's basically just to differentiate different perspectives or different points of understanding and realization from one another; because although this concept of "Wizard" is often thrown around, even at Grade-I, in terms of just *anyone* that operates "magick." When we're applying it within the Mardukite paradigm and its Systemology, we're referring to an individual that has actually worked—already worked—their way *through* the Master-Levels; has already *been* a Master and is working at "Wizard Levels" beyond that.

And this isn't to *bait* you, necessarily, unto like: "Oh, well, these 'Wizard Grades' are where it all is and so never mind all this..." The actual fundamentals, all of the development, what is actually *done* to get an individual to a point *of* what we consider, for example, "Wizard Level-0," is *actually* found in Grade-III material. Whether or not this can be *applied* to the same extent that it can be understood as simply a Master-Level of understanding of the knowledge and instruction and the duplication of the instruction—those are two different things.

We're dealing with a level *now*, which most trip and stumble over—even the lower levels of Mind Tech or Magic Tech—that, I mean, what we're dealing with *now*, we're dealing with actual applications and we're gonna be dealing with ways in which people are using the stuff that we've only alluded to up until this point; but these are actual applications of ancient mysticism—ancient wisdom—that surpass what has been given to us prior.

Even our understanding of the "Infinity of Nothingness"—this concept in the direction of "AN"; the direction towards the "Alpha" existence—that there is an "Infinity of Nothingness" that exists outside the boundaries of what we even conceive to be the "Spiritual Existence" or anything that falls in the domain of the "Mental Planes" or the "Astral" work and whatnot. This has been one of those facets that has actually befuddled the philosophers and mystics alike in the past.

When we're defining the parameters, or what's intended by our Standard Model of Systemology, it's important to note that this "sphere"—this encompassing sphere—of the "All" in the direction of "AN" (which is the Spiritual Universe of the Alpha Existence), which is for our purposes when we are looking at it from *this* point, the more "metaphysical" or composed of more "spiritual energy" and "spiritual matter" —in and of itself is not dependent on the Physical Universe, the universe here in the beta-existence, the "physical energy" and "physical matter" to exist.

These two universes, or these two *parameters* of universe, because they may each in themselves—the Alpha states and Beta states—these may have multiple divisions within themselves; there may be other "beta-existences." But as they are concerned, in terms of energy, when we are talking about the Alpha Spirit operating through the Spiritual planes and have *effect* or a *Point-of-View* of *Awareness* in the physical or in beta-existence, there is only *one* point of connectivity.

And we use the term "ZU-line" in Mardukite Zuism—but, it's essentially, it's the *Life* or *Awareness* of the Alpha Spirit or individual; and what they are considering *for and as Self*, their *point-of-view* as *Self*.

An individual could easily extend a *Lifeline* to a "genetic vehicle" or an "organic body" *as* a point of contact or even to communicate, or you know, to *carry* its own *Awareness* and interact in a beta-existence or the Physical Universe—but it *doesn't* to mean it *has* to be *entrapped* into one. And unfortunately given all of the heavy conditioning—the heavy weights around, even the "mental system" tied directly to physical existence and our considerations of operating a "genetic vehicle"—this is considered far and above what is treated in other aspects of, for example, a "cord" or a "line" with the "astral body" or anything of that nature.

With out *logic* we have to, again, assume that with our consideration of the required facets of manifestation, or the properties of manifestation, that the only point—the connective point—for existence or for manifestation in the Physical Universe *is* the "ZU-line" or, for example, the *individual*; the actual Spiritual Lifeline that's extended between —that is actually the point of Awareness, or what we say 'the Observer' of what is being manifested.

Our Standard Model is also—when we take it one step farther, we have, you know, we've already divided the "circle" into this *smaller* circle with Physical existence, beta-existence, being *down here*—and Alpha... We then put the "ZU-line" across it; and it gives us this idea that there's this point of contact that runs from, basically, *zero* and *Infinity* on this scale, or on this Model.

And so we consider gradients of that—and what we ended up actually applying to it directly, was the *Sevenfold System* of Mesopotamia, the *seven-plus-one* system, which is reflected in the stepped-levels of the physical "*ziggurat*" temples of Babylonia—and, of course, corresponding "Gate" symbolism that represent spiritual levels of Awareness or various states of defragmentation, or Self-purification, as one would *ascend* toward the direction of "AN" with this *Pathway of Self-Honesty.*

And this was kind of like in a reflection of the "*footsteps of the gods.*" Of course, this could go in either direction. But, it was in reflection of *our own* personal fragmentation, that by working our way through *up* these steps of it—almost in the "*footsteps of the gods*" [laughs] that we would be able to reach points of increasing *defragmentation*; to basically undo what has been done.

When you place this *over* the Standard Model, you end up with these "tiers"—these "seven tiers"—with the "circle" of the beta-existence being halfway up the line. When you draw the line down the middle of it, halfway up the line is the division between the "smaller circle" and the "larger circle." And what we have there is essentially, if we divide them into equal parts, you end up with "4."

So, we have "1" "2" "3" "4" going up this line, occupying *within* beta-existence and then "5" "6" "7" going through this larger Alpha circle, and then of course reaching "8" as the Infinity point—the point where it meets the "Infinity of Nothingness."

This isn't necessarily—just like there's the "Kabbalah" and representations on a personal level with, for example, the "Chakras" and other sevenfold systems, even the ziggurat and so forth—we're not implying that there's a physical representation of everything; but *this* Model is quite *workable* as we get farther into the Systemology of it and how we've applied it and used it to gauge and actually *reach* different newer level of realization.

This was actually the *Key*—the Standard Model that is represented in Grade-III—*is* the *Key* for that Gate and the application of it. Because, here we are at Grade-III; we're talking about the *Third Gate* now—the Gate of Ishtar; the Gate of Inanna-Ishtar—and we're talking about "Venus"; we're talking about a handling of the Human Condition as it relates to *emotional* reactivity—the bridge between the Mind and the Body being the *emotional* response-mechanisms; what people have referred to as "conditioning" in the past. This "Standard Model" really helps to demonstrate that.

With the development of Grade-III and the Standard Model that we began to actually systematize and order *our* way of looking at the various "Gates" and "tiers" and, basically, lay out the remaining *Pathway to Infinity*—and begin to actually form some kind of structure; and also a semantic vocabulary so that we can be clear in our definitions and how we approached, not only our own understanding of this in contrast to any other former methods used, or uses of terminology and so forth.

Even in the classifications of, for example, the idea that "understanding" and "Awareness"—although they are very similar, they are not exactly the same thing. And so, you know, "understanding" is what we were talking about with an *application* of the various "ledges" of *knowing* or knowledge that we've had at each grade of personal development. These can only be *illuminated* or brought to a practical use, or what people sometimes refer to as "wisdom," in proportion to the level of *Awareness* that's being maintained at the same time.

Honestly, an individual could have a very—a high level of understanding, but if their *Actualized Awareness* is low, the practical application of that *still* is going to bring it *down*, when you're talking about "functional," or you're talking about "actions," or you're talking about response-mechanisms—it's gonna bring it *down* in the level that is *actually* being *activated;* or in many cases, being stimulated by the environment, or being handled—or *not* being handled—within the control of the individual.

Prior to the inclusion of "Grades"—because "Systemology" begins its own stand-alone pattern of work and information—and so, prior to that, we are basically dealing with levels; and so, what we were doing is defining various levels based on this sevenfold pathway—and "1" through "4" being the range or parameter of the Human Condition—and applying everything we could, in terms of what lined up concerning "mysticism," various aspects of "occultism," "religion," "philosophy," "psychology"—all of this—to basically get a better understanding for how this Model could be set up and applied.

Of course, when we realized we were treating also *Awareness* levels, it became clear that this Standard Model could be applied not only to "cosmology" and the experience of various "Universes," but also be *actual*, from Source, the individual being the "Observer," *how* this could be calculated along the way—whether an individual is operating within specific *emotional* levels or had particular *mental* fragmentation, or the ways in which the Mind and Emotion were connected—these could all be charted and gauged and understood relative to this "Standard Model" and understanding *its* relationship with the Human Condition.

And so, this is where "Systemology"—it begins to become its *own* field of "science," its own study; it's connected to its own "spiritual religious" system, for example, "Mardukite Zuism"—but, the two are actually... We have two different "committees" or two different "divisions" that are actually working on that. "Mardukite Systemology" and the "Systemology Society" is being developed, now, off of this book —"*The Systemology Handbook*"—from one side of our organization. And then, "Mardukite Zuism" and the application of Grade-II and Grade-III combined to create a "modern standard" for "Mesopotamian Neopaganism" and the basic spiritual advisement and counseling of that, is being treated by a completely separate division of our organization.

So, right now, the "Mardukite Academy of Systemology"—which is dispensing the knowledge—is one aspect of it. We have "The Joshua Free Imprint" handling the publications. We have the "Systemology Society" doing the discovery and research attached to the development of the *higher* "Wizard Grades." And we have the "Founding Church of Mardukite Zuism" focused on the development of the Mesopotamian Neopagan and more traditional "religious" elements of this.

This is what is taking place now. And this is what Grade-III represents—it represents the bridge to these higher-level activities that are now happening presently and are still currently in development and presented and also carried throughout the world by individuals that are also, basically, forming the seeds of how they are going to take this stuff farther as well—all within or under the umbrella of the "Mardukite" name.

: LECTURE 39—THE ORIGINAL THESIS :
(September 28, 2020)

Grade-III "Mardukite Systemology"—and the evolution of it as it continues—basically, is a consequence subsequent to the application my "original thesis" on Systemology, which is a composition of multiple essays and papers that was being presented to the underground "*Systemological Society*" nearly a decade ago.

A lot of the original work once used by "*Moroii ad Vitam*"—or *still* used, though that's mainly an underground niche—of which the materials for that are a supplement, I guess, since they are not a part of the Mardukite Master Course; that would be "*The Vampyre's Handbook*" that we publish. Now, a combination of *those* individuals and the incessant application of my "*Original Thesis*" of Systemology *to* the Grade-II work ended up resulting in, *finally*, "*The Tablets of Destiny*" nearly a year ago, which is "*Liber-One*"—really the public inception—of what took nearly a decade of underground work to establish as "Mardukite Systemology."

Although, it's not—it's something that's used for "posterity." We don't really require, for example, an individual to have read "*The Original Thesis*" in order to understand "*The Tablets of Destiny*" or to apply the material in "*Crystal Clear*" to their life. However, for purposes of having a "Master" understanding of how this all developed and what this all entails, it *is* all included in your Grade-III textbook, "*The Systemology Handbook.*"

"*The Original Thesis*" basically applied a *philosophy* to just a general universalistic understanding of the Human Condition. It was definitely of a "Mardukite" flavor, because, of course, it incorporated the idea of the ancient Anunnaki, the establishment of civilization and its progression—as we've been able to cover it in this course. But, it was mainly a *philosophy*.

It wasn't until we *crossed* this philosophy numerous times with the ancient cuneiform texts, which we refer to numerous times as the Arcane Tablets, that we were able to get any kind of *workable* effective system out of this. And this, of course, spawned "Mardukite Systemology," which has actually been able to develop at a pretty exponential rate, as a result of finally breaking through (with) these *Keys*.

It's ironic, because what we are talking about in Grade-III is the "Ishtar Gate," and so, the level of—I've made jokes in the past about "getting beyond the Ishtar Gate"; that it was something that just didn't seem to have happened anywhere, as far as recorded history, in terms of traditions and the preservation of any of these systems, as far as how "actualized" the various "initiates" and followers really were.

The big *goal* at this juncture was always about *breaking through* the Ishtar Gate and actually being able to surpass the point of initial "beta-fragmentation" (as it) concerns, for example, to emotional reactivity and all of these "pre-patterned" forms of behavior that seemed to override and take over our sensibilities, or our ability to command our experience as *Self*, and actually be Self-Directed and Self-Determined through and through.

So, it was at *that* point, for example, in delivering to that point, the Grade-III material, that we finally capped off the Mardukite Master Course; because, what else is it but, you know, a gradient of Self-Mastery. And so, that's where we're at.

In it's original presentation, the first booklet is referred to "*Human, More Than Human*" and honestly, even to this day, probably less than one-hundred individuals have been able to acquire, or actually own, this small booklet; because we were only distributing Systemology work to the under ground at that time—and we weren't really publicizing it. We were more focused at the time—until 2019—on the other material; the Grade-I and Grade-II material as entry-points, meanwhile behind-the-scenes, building up this inertia for Mardukite Systemology.

The catch phrase for this—and the pamphlet for it—and the way we've even reintroduced *"The Tablets of Destiny"* when we were promoting it a year ago was that: "The Universe exists within a Sea of Infinity, an ocean of pure potentiality. Do you know your place? Sealed within the Human Condition is a unique life program special to you. Unlock the power of your true identity and live the life you were meant to, Self-honestly as a Free Spirit within NexGen Systemology."

"And what we discovered—or rediscovered—is not a *new* methodology, but the *first* one: the archetypal System of Systems known to the ancients. We used it. We applied the acid test of reality—and only the truth remained. We saw it first hand; beneath the veils and levels and layers of the systems... only the truth remained."

And therein, I launched my *"Original Thesis"*—booklets that were composing my *"Original Thesis"*—and trying to drive the direction of "metahuman" or *homo novus*, this next level of Awareness and Realization and Beingness, that seemed to be only scraped upon or alluded to in all these former systems and traditions and methods of "mysticism" and so forth; but of which has never seemed to be obtained or never seemed to be able to be delivered—never to *my* satisfaction.

There was always this allusion that "well, there might be something in the afterlife; or if you do good now, well good things will eventually happen to you" or something of this respect. But, other than all this "morals and dogma," there didn't seem to be any delivery to any point; no one seemed to be any *happier* for the fact that they were actually working through whatever it is they were working through—they were always still lost in their own fragmentation and operating on various imprinting and so forth.

So, what I was really trying to establish in "*Human, More Than Human*" is the idea that humans are *more than* human; I mean, it's kinda given in the title. And this has been kind of joked about in the past, by those that have commented on it, about how blatantly forthright some of this really was.

But again, it was still being given as kind of a—it could still be taken kind of "tongue in cheek"—with a "Well, we've kind of all known *that*, but then we've been told we *have a soul* and there's spiritual forces at war and then we go to Heaven or we go to Hell" and so forth.

Well—[*sniffs*]—I really didn't find any of that to be the case within our Systemology. *But*, I did find that an individual *was* "soul," *was* "spirit," *was* "I-AM," *was* the "Alpha" of this other existence, and that any of this other stuff that had been attached to it *was* basically *that*: energies and masses and fragments, memories, different emotional encoding, implants, that had been *attached* to the individual.

It was *those things* that were weighing down the quality of the Spirit, the quality of what they were considering "soul." *But*, it isn't like an individual "had" one; like, they were carrying it around in their pocket or something like that—but that is what the individual actually *was*, and that is what we consider the "Alpha Spirit" in Systemology.

And the other concepts introduced in the very beginning of "*The Original Thesis*" is this very idea of "fractioning" of reality—that there's separations—and that these separations are what an individual has a sense of, but it creates more—as the separations take more and more hold as more and more fragmentation is basically standing in the way of a clear view of a clear channel between Self and its own experience—that's when an individual begins to feel more *solemn*, they feel more *hollow*, there's a certain *sadness* that takes over, they become more *introverted*.

Now we're not—when we say *introverted*, we don't mean someone that has the ability to, you know, "self-analyze" or "look within" or be able to observe their own behavior or correct patterns of the Mind and so forth—but an "introverted person" that's just basically *withdrawn* from their interaction with energies, their interaction with flows and energies, the social environment and so forth. This is one of the things that seems to *dim* along with the decline of *Actualized Awareness*.

It's kind of—it's a feeling of *apprehension* and *anxiety*, it's all these these things kind of inherent into the Human Condition that have actually—that are a *part* of this. And this is one of the things that we've actually been *seeking* to resolve; we finally resolved it in Grade-III and our advanced work—but it took *ten years* after "*The Original Thesis*" for this to happen with any kind of *effective results* that could be *duplicated* or *instructed*.

The other thing pointed out in "*Human, More Than Human*" is about the "standard issue" state of a Human being basically just going about their everyday lives *believing* they're "Self-directed" and *believing* they're "Self-determined" and that they are actually experiencing life and everything with clarity, but that there is actually so much artificial programming and fragmentation and "conditioning" taking place—and control over the mental imagery, the associations of knowledge, all of the emotional responses that are attached to experience and former encounters with different facets of life—that really get in the way of that.

So, what we basically question when we're approaching Mardukite Systemology and we're approaching, for example, even the "processing" in Systemology—and, although we won't be getting into the "*piloted processing*" (because we've basically reserved that, the type of management and communication and so forth, to Mardukite Ministers and Pilots that are trained specifically in that) which is beyond the Mardukite Master Course aspects, but...

The purpose of *"Crystal Clear"*—because we knew it was going to take a while to establish [*laughs*] any kind of "piloting program" or to get really a lot of the "Ministry" and different elements of "clergy" and "Zuism" on the road—is that *"Crystal Clear"* is really meant to be a *"self-processing"* guide, although it can be used quite effectively along with piloting. But it was really meant to be a self-processing guide that an individual could use on their own—and so *that* definitely *does* fall within the realm of the Mardukite Master Course and is within the pages of *"The Systemology Handbook,"* so we *will* be dealing with *that* much.

Back when I was writing material for *"The Original Thesis,"* we *didn't* even have "self-processing" available; we didn't have any kind of practical effective aspect to apply until we really spent a lot of time with this. But this is the material that brought us to that state.

A lot of the stuff now—when you start to look at what we did in *"The Tablets of Destiny"* and *"Crystal Clear"*—a lot of the stuff from *"The Original Thesis"* seems very *elementary* and basic, but when we're talking about a Mardukite Master Course or the intellectual-academic level *of* treating Mardukite Systemology as Grade-III within the Academy or the schooling or in your "apprenticeship programs," the material from *"The Original Thesis" is* a fairly accessible introduction, if not using *"The Tablets of Destiny"* directly.

An individual that doesn't really have a background in Mesopotamia, that hasn't worked through Grade-II materials, might actually be able to *reach* a few of the realizations on their own, just by working through the material of *"The Original Thesis"* prior to working with, for example, *"The Tablets of Destiny."*

It's for that reason that I bring this up, because chronologically the inception of Systemology did fall within the domain of—like I said, I started pointing stuff out regarding that in the *"Arcanum"* work; it was always intended even in the 1990's as the upper-levels of, for example, the *"Hermetic Order of the Crystal Dawn"* that we were dealing with at the time.

The whole purpose—or the actual reasoning behind the name "Crystal Dawn" had to do with this same "crystal clarity," the same "metaphors" that we apply all the way up to present day, you know, *twenty years* later with *"Crystal Clear."* That was essentially the functional purpose of the establishment of the "Crystal Dawn" project back in the late 1990's.

Timing is everything. I mean, I didn't even have *"Arcanum"* or any of the graded work that we're doing—that we have accessible—now at the Mardukite Master Course level to actually bridge into this kind of understanding. All I was really dealing with then was a lot of Grade-I work and the individuals that were around me—the ones I was encountering, for example, in the "New Age" marketplaces and bookstores and so forth, were still working at that level.

The rest of them, those that were considered the "Lightworkers" and those that dealt with "Eastern Spirituality" and "chakras" and whatnot, they seemed to be pretty much, you know, attached to their own paradigms with that—and their own understanding and their own work—but were still not *quite* breaking through to find effective means of *really releasing* from the Human Condition fully.

It's really that element—the idea of the Human Condition being something *separate* from *Self*, separate from I-AM, that is actually one of the pinnacles of a Grade-III realization. This is something that the former levels of understanding or the former Grades are not necessarily impressing fully. They kind of make it seem like, "Well, you're this being or an Awareness and when you die you just float around as this ghostly being and so forth" or "your shackled to one of these or another afterlives." These are artificial beliefs; they're attached only to certain "religions" and so forth; they don't necessarily have any other basis in fact.

In the language of Grade-III, when we're talking about "*encoding*," we're talking about the *emotional* level of "*imprinting.*" And this is what, in the past, or in psychology or in other philosophies, we might refer to as "conditioning." And then, when we're talking about thought, when we're talking about beliefs—when we're talking about the associative knowledge that an individual has with the actual understanding that they're maintaining with the world around them—we're talking about basic mental programming; we're talking about the Mind at that point.

And the "Mind" and the "Body" *communicate* essentially through the stimulation of biochemicals—and so, what we find is that there's certain [*laughs*] basically like "push-button" mechanisms attached to the Human Condition, where it can be "conditioned" or "fragmented" or "controlled" and "manipulated" or given false knowledge based on the *encoding* of either "*pleasure*" and "*pain.*"

We see a lot of imprinting and fragmentation attached to points of, for example, *pain*, or in other elements, *loss*—any sense of suffering on the individual; because, you're talking about *that* individual's experience from *within* that Body, and the more that happens, the individual begins to *feel*, the individual begins to start *thinking as*—the programming all comes from within, *interior* of the Mind-Systems and the Human Condition, the parameters of beta-existence.

The more an individual, for example, feels pain, and isn't able to really able to confront or face the nature of that—or maintain control over that experience—they begin to become more and more the *effect* of, for example, their experience of the Human Condition. They begin to associate more and more of what they believe Self or I-AM *is* with the Human Condition.

In the past, this has been treated only loosely in some like "regressive" techniques and certain forms of "creative psychology" and so forth; but, it's never really been brought into the level of "mysticism" or being treated at, for example: just last week we were talking about "ritual magic," we were talking about "Anunnaki"—potentially "alien gods" and things, you know, for the last few days—and now we're talking about ways of basically relieving the suffering of the Human Condition enough to get an individual to *free* their considerations outside, the fact that they're not their body.

Now, when we talk about things like the "Matrix-System"—I mean, now today, this is another example where we have certain pieces of *inspired* science-fiction media and so forth, which kind of demonstrate a certain understanding or at least give *examples*—tangible examples for concepts—that many many years ago would be hard to explain, hard to understand for people.

For example, this concept of a "Matrix"—we know of a "matrix" as like a "grid." The "grid" implies action in multiple directions, so we're talking about a *duality*—we're talking about systems that basically operate energy flows based on the fact that they are a polarity. We kind of touched on that when we were approaching the idea on "why is there polarity and dualism and the fragmentation of universes" and whatnot, connected to "Necronomicon Revelations" (*in our lectures earlier this morning*) when wrapping up Grade-II. This is one of those points where the Grades intermix.

Ironically, a lot of the work for "*The Original Thesis*" was being developed simultaneously with the year that "*Liber-R*" and such was being developed; because again, "*Liber-9*" and "*Liber-R*" and that culmination of work that was meant to cap off the "Mardukite Core" at the time, was actually meant to lead right into *this*; and chronologically it *did*, we just didn't publicize it very much, because it was still fairly in development.

Unlike in Grade-I, where an individual is given all of these "ritual" demonstrations; and Grade-II, where you have all of these "religious" and "traditional" ramifications and the "Ordering of the Cosmos" and different things—we want to be able to at least establish some kind of practical "spiritual tech" in order to *deliver* this concept. So, it kind of laid dormant on back-burners and being worked on quietly and only a few individuals for nearly a decade.

But, we're talking about the "Matrix"—we're talking about a visible series of lights, the "array," the "light-matrix"—the System—that basically is what you can see; what is around, what is given substance. And an individual participates in this regularly. That is one of the functions of the Alpha Spirit: that they can *create*—if nothing else, they can *create* the imagery within their own Universe.

This is what is basically being "snap-shot" around us—we, you know, there is a certain sense of newness or "novelty" when we discover something or see something for the first time; and there is a certain *imprint* that takes place, which kind of dulls our Awareness thereafter, when we basically lead off the imprint.

So, you've got a certain—an encounter takes place. It's basically just energy. Then experience takes over—the parameters of what the senses can experience; the Human Condition can take over; and then all of this is given a classification. And so the next time an individual encounters the "same" thing, there is a certain energy signature—key waves and frequencies that are picked up—and rather than give it the full sense of attention that you would when something was new, we get basically just a replay—we get basically just the snap-shots that have been taken, and thrown up at us and that's basically what we are experiencing.

A lot of times, this is what causes the "world around us" to kind of "cave in"—because we aren't really (consciously) participating in its creation anymore; we've just basically passed on that responsibility. Although we are still creating it, we're creating it just on basic pictures and imprints and snap-shots; the way in which we've assigned values to things before so that they just kind of fade into the background.

The second text that was developed—the second booklet that was released for *"Systemology: The Original Thesis"*—was called: *"Defragmentation."* Again, a very self-explanatory title concerning the nature—after having established the nature of the Alpha Spirit in *"Human, More Than Human,"* the *"Defragmentation"* booklet was about, basically, getting back to that point.

This is where Self as an Awareness Point or Total Consciousness is treated as the I-AM or the "Alpha Free Spirit" and that a Self-Honest experience of the I-of-Self *is* the only *True Identity* and the only *True Point-of-View* of the Observer. This would be the most basic, prime, *Alpha*—state of Self.

Programming—and what some have called "conditioning"—or encoding, is what dictates the systems that rule fragmentation. And, of course, you have a material existence, since it is consciousness-created, it is fragmented and developed by these creative Alpha Spirits; and we are *all* participating in doing this.

Basically, these systems are composed of fragmented parts; and then, of course, they work and are interrelated to each other—and that's where we start to deal with this idea that what we're dealing with is called "Systemology." Because even when we're talking about traditions and different paradigms and all of the ways in which this ancient wisdom has extended to us, you would have modern systems that are essentially fragments of an ancient wisdom.

Each is, like, growing a branch off of a singular tree—and we work our way back and we ended up, again, in Mesopotamia. So, having traversed 6,000 years of lore and knowledge and information and culture and *systems*—and all of these fragments—we've finally been able to resolve that "Mystery" and basically just see it all for what it *is*, and then we've worked past that, working into Mardukite Systemology.

And here we start to treat the nature of systems, systems operating within each other, larger systems operating upon smaller ones—kind of "*cog-wheel*" aspects and dynamics; and that's what it is, is "*dynamic systems.*"

But, this isn't—it's not the mechanistic "clockwork" universe as a lot of physics would have you believe; it's *dynamic systems*, where each one—it's not just "billiard balls" (hitting) against "billiard balls." There's other forces and other elements that work upon that. All of which mainly relate to the individual.

I mean, the individual is the one that is basically able to tip the scale on that. Yeah, we would have a very "clockwork" mechanistic universe *were it not* for the fact that there is *Life* in this Universe—and *Life* has the ability to *change* things, to *create* things, to *destroy* things; and all of these are not parameters that are necessarily totally fixed. I mean, how can can predict if someone were just to suddenly leap across a room or whatnot.

There's no mechanistic "cog" definition that applies to the individual; and this is what has separated, for example, *our* Systemology and what has kept "religion" and "science" at various odds, is that most of the material sciences can only really be concerned with the material *objective* universe as it applies *almost* free of the Observer; but since it cannot do that, it's always impinging upon it its own expectations, its own observations and, of course, the limits that sensory organs or the perceptions or what have you—the limits that it's able to define its *causal effects*.

Because, that's what we're dealing with: *cause* and *effect*, pretty much at all points here; we're dealing with an individual trying to be as much at *cause* as possible over their experience of reality, over their creation and direction of energies and so forth—as opposed to becoming the *effect* and slowly *succumbing* to all of these forces of this material universe, which will definitely, if allowed to—you know, it's a *hungry* universe—it will definitely take over, if allowed.

When we talk about "programmed-identity-personas" or "*phases*," we're talking about, like, these "*personalities*" that act as "filters" in which to view the world; we're talking about, from the perspective of the "Mind-System," these are the filters that, as the Human Condition, they're embedded with *emotional* energies, they have their own harmonic *resonance*, they have their own *inclinations* as to what is considered attractive and what is considered repulsive.

And by putting one of them "on," by having these filters "on," you end up actually filtering—you filter more of the experience and that *validates* the filters and basically makes things more solid. So, experience becomes reality and reality becomes experience; and then *emotional encoding* and the *memory imprinting* and all of that determine what the definitions or parameters of that reality experience are—as they are perceived.

This is basically what constitutes, like I said, the experience of *Life*, the *Universe* and *Everything*; and at a "philosophical" level, this stuff all seems, you know, real *easy*... it all seems to make sense. But *still*, it took ten years to bring it to anything practical; primarily the best example of that being the material in "*Crystal Clear.*"

Even in that sense, we talk about the distortions or the fragmentation of an individual right *in* the text of *"Defragmentation"* from *"The Original Thesis"* as "crystalline distortions"—distortions in the perception; basically, these pre-programmed *compulsions, obsessions, tendencies,* what are classified falsely as "disorders" and "phobias." And that's one of the issues I always had; because, to be honest, I also have an academic background in "psychology"—I don't just speak of these things or it isn't that I didn't pursue (traditional) psychology because of a lack of *awareness* of it. Unfortunately, most psychology is no longer (dealing) with anything about "consciousness"—its only concerned with "behaviors."

And the other reason being that, like, taking a look at the *"DSM-IV"*—it's this diagnostic manual that you use in psychology concerning mental health and mental behavior—really, it's just a bunch of classifications; it's just a bunch of definitions. Every little quirk that an individual has, or could potentially have, is somehow in there and classifiable as a "disorder" and so forth.

But, there's really no methodology behind *correcting* any of this—that's never been established; nor (has) there ever, within that paradigm of "mental health," ever been an establishment of what *"sanity"* actually is—or when an individual is finally *"done,"* for example, with their "therapy." Because most of the time it's just this ongoing thing. An individual that is the type that can respond well to that will invariably just continue feeding the bank of the psychologist indefinitely—never actually achieve a point of where they feel *Self-Actualized*. That point of Beingness never seems to get returned to the patient, in the traditional medical sense of this work.

That's why we take this up in the sense of a "spirituality" and the "religion" of Mardukite Zuism *and* a pursuit of a *higher* level of "metaphysics" and so forth, because honestly, there's no reason for me to endeavor into the fields of "medicine" and "psychology" and interfere with the realms of "doctors" because, we're not even in the same realm.

We're treating a *Spirit*, which they've no longer acknowledged even *exists*—as far as their practices are concerned. We're dealing with the *Mind*, which because it's not fixed strictly to the "brain" as an "organ" as far its actual existence—yeah, sure it uses the "brain organ"—but, because they were never able to find the "I-AM" or Alpha Spirit, because they were never able to find "consciousness" and put it under the microscope, because they've never been able to define the "Mind" and actually be able to determine what it is, for example, independent of the brain as a physical organ, *none* of that stuff exists in the realm of physical sciences and psychology. Our domain and their domain do not seem to overlap in any way shape or form, except for the fact that, well, you can kind of classify the knowledge in the same vicinity many times.

These "crystalline distortions" can become *crystal clear*, when this crystalline catalyst, for example, the "function machine" that I was referring to in an *earlier* lecture—whatever is being used by the Mind-System to process the energetic transmission of information; if this is crystal clear of fragmentation, then the experience can be.

You can see the *effects* in everyday life of just what external fragmentation programming actually—and the encoding—leads to, in terms of the Human Condition. You see a lot of people with irrational or erratic or completely chaotic thought; the inability to concentrate or focus—the kind of fatigue and irritability that seems to plague the Human Condition more and more everyday; and of course, this increased attention on ailments and diseases of the body. This all affects what we're treating or looking towards in Mardukite Systemology as a "Self-Honest" experience.

That's what we're trying to correct even within Grade-III and our application of the work and the milestones that we consider capped off with Grade-III, because as much as one uses the *nomenclature* or the concept of "Wizards" and what not, no real "Wizard" work can be done until we get a person back up to *zero*; back up to at least a point of—you know, even though they are occupying the Human Condition, they are not completely trapped by all of the "push–pull" mechanism that are attached to that.

And the [*mechanisms*] have been picked up along the way and what they've been treating as an experience—that they have a real need to hold onto, because without holding onto that experience, they feel like they don't *have* something. And so, this concept of *loss*, the programmed conditioning about *loss*, it's really what keeps many people from letting things go—old ideas, old energetic masses, the inability to forgive, the inability to look at something new.

Like in "*objective processing*," we might have an object on the table—we get an individual to look at it as if practically for the first time with full awareness, over and over again, to be able to duplicatively do that. We treat this kind of stuff at higher levels of "Systematic Processing" and it yields results, because we're looking at the highest-level application of all these little *rites* and *lores* and *rituals* and *pathways*—and all this stuff that's come before—we looked at the highest-level of what we could apply to that and what it might do, and therein we found Mardukite Systemology.

All of this was really based on the materials that are found in "*The Original Thesis.*" At this juncture—I mean, we're working on other introductory materials and point of entry that could be used; inexpensive, easy-to-read, easy-to-understand, *entry points* into Systemology, that you could dispense or *disseminate* and disperse and assist in bringing people up to this higher-level. But, up unto that point, "*The Original Thesis*" was pretty much *it*. And then, again, as an evolution of a Grade-II, "*The Tablets of Destiny*" book that came out a year ago, which is within "*The Systemology Handbook*," that is an incredible bridge from wherever someone's *been* to wherever they *can be*, and wherever we are now, with Mardukite Systemology at Grade-III.

: LECTURE 40—THE STANDARD MODEL :
(September 28, 2020)

The Standard Model of Systemology actually evolved over the course of a decade and is something of great interest, because it's not only the standard on which we apply all of our systemological *logic* and reasoning, the way in which we gauge our *processing*, the way in which we've charted the *Pathway to Infinity*.

It's also alluded to in the Mardukite Master Course lectures throughout—that there's many relationships between these various systems of understanding what has later evolved from, for example, the material in Babylon, to the various factions; whether it be the Kabbalah or the way that the *"ziggurat" Ladder of Lights* has been interpreted, or the various connections to these *zones* and the Chakras as being the veils that *fix* the various levels to the Human Condition, or of *Self*, various energetic bodies and so forth.

There's many ways in which these have been applied. But, for our purposes, the systematic way in which they are analyzed for Mardukite Systemology is considered the "Standard Model of Systemology." Although there's elements of it given throughout the *older* works—even in the old *"Reality Engineering"* lectures and so forth—it was not *fine-tuned* until the delivery of the first, *"Liber-One,"* the volume *"The Tablets of Destiny,"* which also is, of course, included in your *"Systemology Handbook."*

Now, the Standard Model consists of the concentric rings—the circles—of the standard *cosmological* model, in addition to the "ZU-line" of individual experience and *Awareness* laid over that. In a lot of the *earlier* texts, when we were even just developing it in the last year, we would refer to it often times as the "Standard Model *and* ZU-line."

Really, the Standard Model and ZU-line are, kind of, *one*. It's just that they were developed independently. One was developed in regard to the energetic qualities and states and conditions of Universes and existences; and the other being the variation in frequency between the "I-AM" or Alpha-Spirit or *Self* and the interactions with those other various states.

So, when you have the *cosmological* model and the Spheres of Existence and so forth; and then you take the ZU-line and its associations and put that over it—you get the full Standard Model of Systemology on which we've been able to not only establish the Grade-III curriculum, but also move forward in... that was one of the... It was essentially the *Master Key* to accessing these *higher* Gates of Realization that have surpassed our *Awareness* as the Human Condition for thousands and thousands of years.

I mean, this is what the pursuits and the goals were all aimed toward—but it seemed we were always falling back or falling away from the goal, or being diverted from the proper path, every time it seemed that Humanity or a system or a tradition might break through.

Now, technically the "ZU-line" as a *Life Energy*, as an *Awareness* of existence, the individual as *Self*, the Spiritual "I-AM" exists—it's a continuum that from Infinity to Infinity. And so, even though at the Grade-III level that it's demonstrated that we're working with a Standard Model of Systemology the way it's given there: a *zero-point* to *Infinity*, which is represented by "8." And of course, that just logically follows anyways, because you turn the "8" on its side and you got an Infinity symbol—the Arabic numeral of "8" anyways.

If you follow the line down in any of the times that I've drawn it, you'll see there's an Infinity below the *zero-point* representing the *continuity* of the Physical Universe. We don't really deal with the "sub-levels"—the "sub-zero" levels—of *Awareness* on the ZU-line, in terms of (the) Grade-

III Standard Model, but it should be at least known, because it comes up with—"Uh, Infinity? Or Zero? What is this?" [*laughs*]

It should be known that *Infinity* is *always* "Infinity"—gradients to it, we have, for example, classifications for "minus-one" or "minus-five" or whatever, on the Standard Model—but this is actually introduced at Grade-IV, so lies outside the Mardukite Master Course. There is *enough* material within Grade-III just dealing with the *side* of the Standard Model—the "positive" end of the Standard Model—that concerns manifestations and existences in the Universe, not the *withdrawal* of the Alpha-Spirit, which is what the other end of the Model basically pertains to.

Until we get to that point, there's plenty to work with and deal with here at Grade-III, and all of the material in the Grade-III textbook—"The Systemology Handbook." But, it does come up—and in actually giving the lecture; and the transcript for it in *"Crystal Clear"*—but in giving the lecture for *"Crystal Clear"* [*laughs*], I was actually *asked* about this, because that's when I was really perfecting the application of using the Standard Model in regards to "processing" and so yeah, it kinda already comes up in Grade-III and there's answers for that; we just tend to treat it more at the *higher* levels.

At "0" on the Standard Model, we're dealing with the continuity of the Physical Universe—basically, *matter* as condensed energy. So, in regards to where—so, if you're talking about the *"zero-point"* of the continuity, the *All-ness* of what is considered "physical matter" and "physical objects"—inert matter—we're talking about the *zero-point* (for *beta-existence*) of the Standard Model. We're talking about the "ZU-line" in the same respect—when laid over it, they overlap there, and that would be considered the same as, for example, *"body-death"* or cellular activity and sensory perceptions have been brought down to "0."

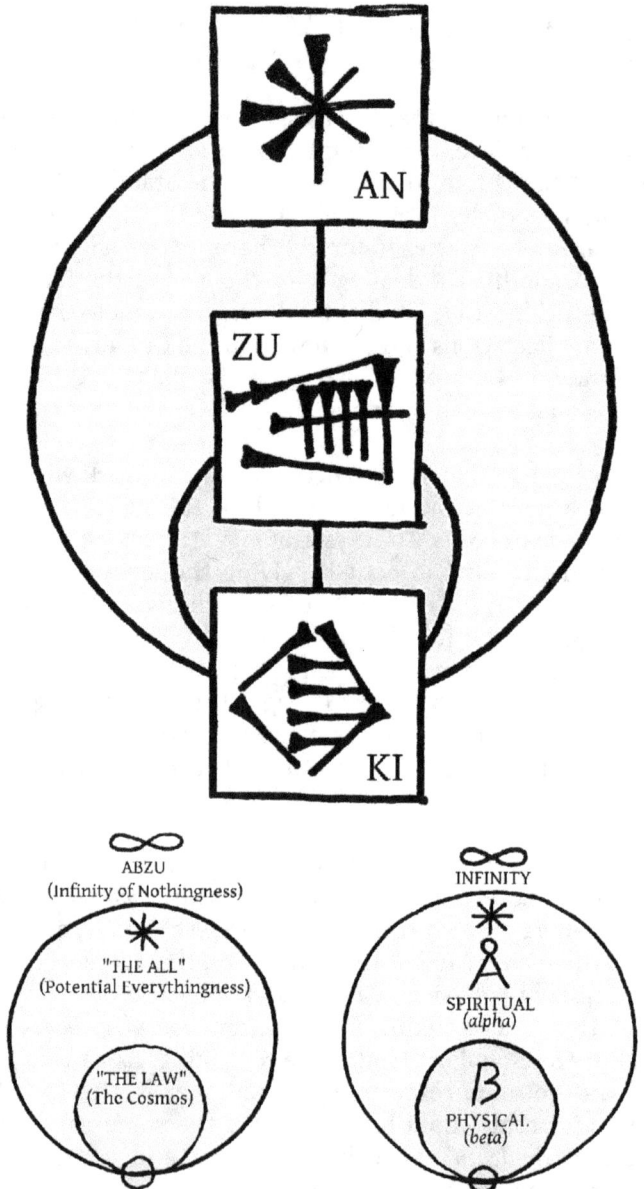

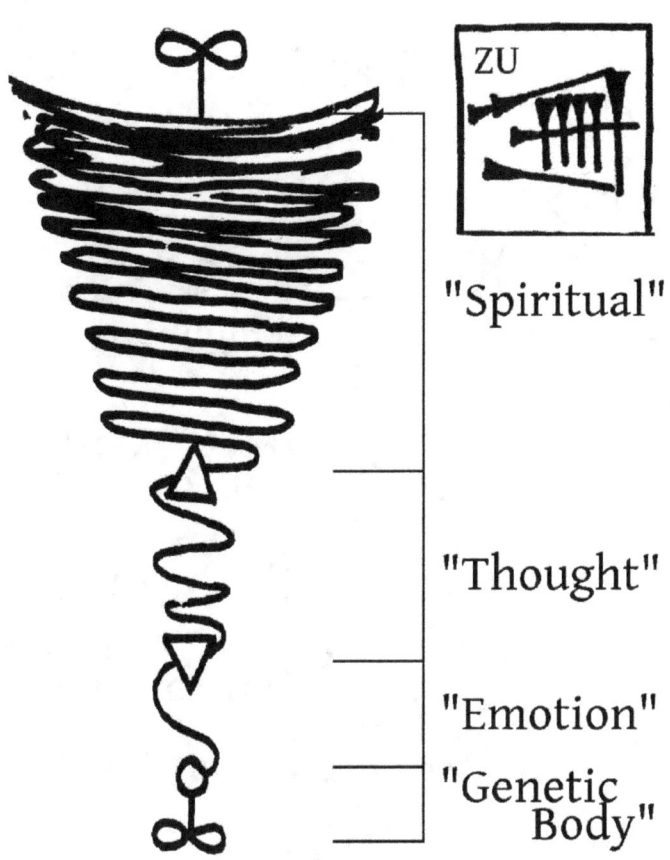

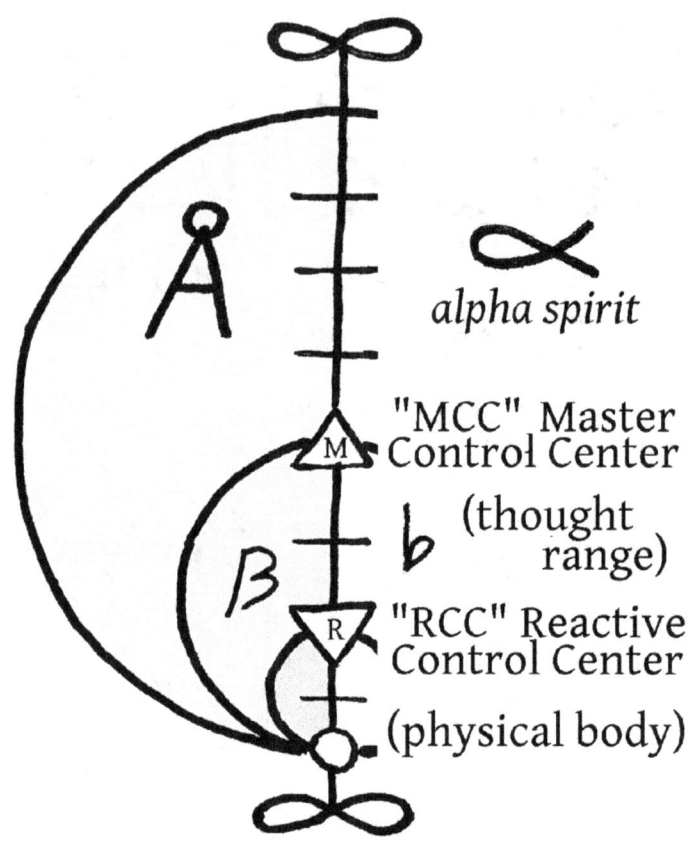

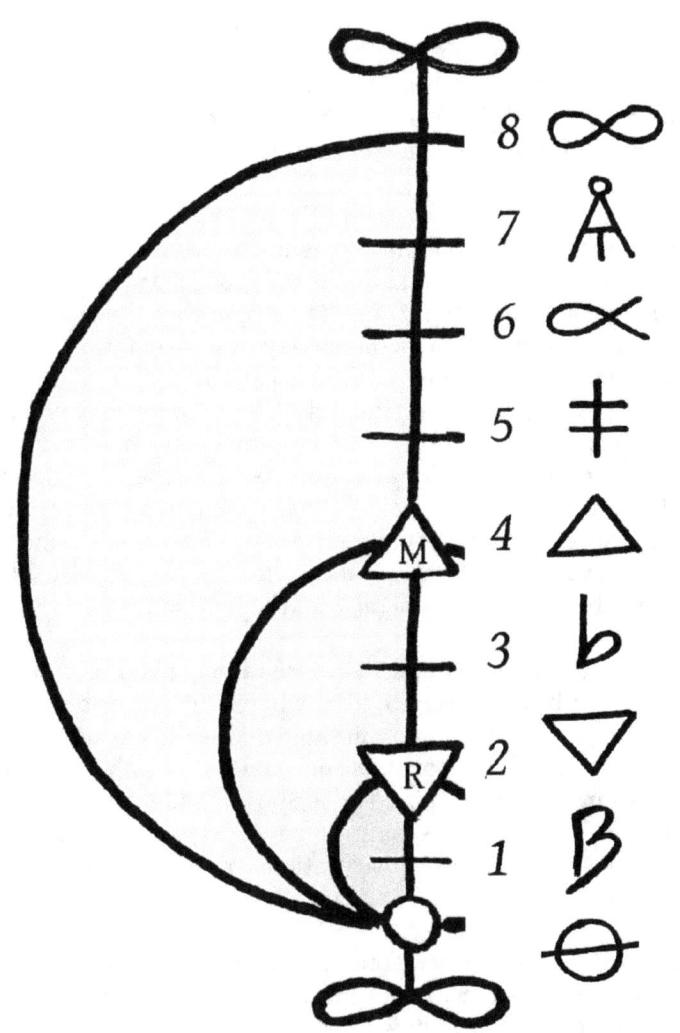

physical "genetic vehicle" has been overwhelmed by the forces—has become such the effect of the forces—of the Physical Universe, that it is just no longer able to sustain.

Of course, this has nothing to do with the continuation of the Spirit that uses it [*the body*]; we're talking about, at the *zero-point*, we're talking about physical bodies as "meat" and the Physical Universe like "rocks." That level.

And then as we move between "0" and "2" on the Standard Model, we're talking about biochemical production that is involved *with* the "genetic organism" but is strongly influenced *by* "mental activity" and it's still within the realm of viewable, because there's many aspects of emotions and chemicals and hormones that you can actually put under the microscope, but unfortunately when you're only treating it from a Grade-I—or a "*Grade-Zero*," you know, a very physical, mundane, point of understanding—then you don't really get very far with that. That's what we talk about, when we're talking about *emotion*. So, between "0" and—well, between "0.00001" [*laughs*] and "2," we're basically talking about the *emotional range* of the individual.

And then between "2" and "4" we're talking about the *mental range* within the Mind-System when you're considered it attached to the Human Condition—whether it's attached to *this* "genetic vehicle" or another "genetic vehicle," you're still talking about a Spirit—or a Spiritual Identity, or the Self, the Alpha-Spirit—using some type of Mind-System that's attached to the considerations of a physical condition.

And so, it's been considered that many elements of this "Mind-System"—some of its most intensive *imprinting* and *fragmentation*—is actually what's carried forward or carried into a new existence or contributes to the way one is selected, for example; or what is *to be* the next considerations of experience for what is to be the next incarnation of *Life*.

We know that many individuals now are looking into things like "tapping into past life memory" or other things, or dealing with "spiritual"—what they consider the (quote; unquote) "*karma*," which is really kind of "Cosmic Law" or "Causal Law," basically just dealing with the energetic flows of reality. But these kind of concepts—the very fact that these kind of concepts are considered at all, this is considered *outside* the domain of "beta-existence." This idea that there's this *Spirit* operating a "Mind-System" that is fixed to these types of considerations.

So, we work through that little by little in "defragmentation processing" until up at the Wizard-Levels. I mean, by Grade-V, we plan to deal with more of "unlocking past life memory" on a *systematic* level, and things like that. At *this* point, we're dealing with enough material here in Grade-III and enough stuff going on with an individual in their *present* life and the things to confront and face-up to in the *present* life, that we try not to get too wrapped up in these higher pursuits.

But, that isn't to say they aren't there and that isn't to say that it's a secret—like, if you're not initiated to some degree that... But, as far as treating it as gradient scale—if you want to be working it up the Pathway, each time... each step—just like these lectures being each on farther towards the reach of the *Gateways to Infinity*.

You're working at it progressively; you're not just trying to jump into it. There's nothing within the material—there's no "magic words"—there's nothing where an individual can *become the effect* of the material enough to *make* the material *effective.* The individual *must* be at cause—must be *knowingly* at cause—each time they are working through this type of work; anything in Systemology.

There's no secret books: we don't limit the releases—I mean, it takes me some time to work them out and make sure their solid. But, we release stuff as it's developed; there's no hidden channels of knowledge here. It's just that, as far as the accessibility or the level of realization an individual is going to get to with it—if they haven't worked through or worked out all of the stuff that stands in the way of that, the reading of the books, or the hearing of the words at some point, are not enough to get an individual there.

If that were the case, all of these efforts of "Self-Help" and "New Thought" and "Law of Mind" and "Science of Mind" and "Law of Attrac..." and all this—if that were enough, we'd see a different state today on the planet than we already do; and that is why we're delivering the Mardukite Master Course.

Because, more than me just sitting up in some "Ivory Tower" and writing a bunch of books and going, "Okay, well, we'll see what happens with that." We're now taking a little bit more—as we go into the 2020's—a more active approach to delivering the information and standardizing it and actually, for example, in this course, *certifying* "Instructors" that have the ability to take these materials and actually deliver results with them—all the way up the Grades—with Seekers; whether it be individually with apprenticeships or with schools and lodges or groups that you decide to form.

Obviously, just like any of the other "mystical" *models* or *symbols*—I mean, the meaning really comes from the significance and the understanding of the individual. There's nothing—there's... even the glyphs and images and different logos and things we develop for Systemology and the way we classify things—none of this in and itself is going to produce the *effect*; it all comes from Self.

The Standard Model of Systemology is—it's just like any other "mystical model." We're using—rather than the partition of the Kabbalistic models of the past, or any other concepts, we're establishing a *new* model; but it's based on all the ancient wisdom, the correct points, the points of synchronicity between them all—all throughout the ages.

This same paradigm is reflected in, for example, the "Ladder of Lights" or "Gates" and other forms of Self-Actualization—anything that deals with "Ascension." We are just—we're actually *systematizing* ours a little bit more thoroughly; and therein, getting a little more effective results when it comes to applying it as an actual Spiritual Tech, and not just a passive philosophy.

So, in *"The Tablets of Destiny"* material—in our *"Liber-One"* material—we're really do focus on the Human Condition as it relates to the "beta-existence." And that's the part of the scale (on the Model) that we're basically treating. The idea that it does 1, 2, 3, 4, 5, 6, 7, 8—and there's all these parameters and various divisions of that and how we classify that; most of that got relayed a little bit more thoroughly in the *"Crystal Clear"* volume.

But, in *"The Tablets of Destiny"* we are concerned with, specifically, kind of dividing the idea that there's this "genetic vehicle," which has its emotional biochemical systems attached to it, that are connected to a Mind-System that controls, and which can also be influenced by it. And this is basically—all these systems and "Control Centers" and so forth, are basically under the command and observation of Self.

And of course, Self is looking down this ZU-line to *project* its sense of *Beingness*—the actual *Awareness* of itself—anywhere along the line. And it is using its filters and receptors and sensors at each step of the way in order to perceive the "environment" or the "frequencies" or whatever aspect—universal or existential aspect—is taking place at that level.

At the point of "4" on the Standard Model, we call it the "Master Control Center" or the "Mind Control Center" and it's basically the point of which the individual—as a Spiritual Being—is treating or commanding or having any kind of, like, avatar-like control *over* the experience of the genetic vehicle in beta-existence.

There are some that have called it the "Higher Self" or so forth—but really, there *is just one Self*. And then there's anywhere along this ZU-line, the *Self* can basically put *its Beingness*—put its point *to Be*—and project as an Awareness to that point. But, the Self is always back up in this Spiritual Alpha zone. It's kind of "looking down" or able to experience anywhere down this conduit or channel or continuum or the ZU-line, and experience these various levels.

We talked about "0" being the inert-matter level—I mean, everything is in motion, but we're basically referring to that as the point of near-static, just as the point of Infinity of Nothingness is meant to be an Absolute, this kind of static existence outside of All; everything else of which is in motion—we find the *zero-point* being this "balancing factor" in beta-existence to where it is this inert non-motion.

Up at "1" we start dealing with more of the *physiological* functions—the kind of, "fight-flight" response-mechanisms of the individual, the ones that are basically being treated at the *lowest* level of heavy emotional syrupy reactive levels. And then at "2" we call that the "Reactive Control Center," which is basically the monitoring system for the response-mechanisms; except it really doesn't monitor very well—it's basically working on a "push–pull" mechanism. It encounters something; it has a certain experience with it—emotionally charged already—and so that is what is treated as reality at that given moment.

And then when we get up to "3" we're talking about "associative thought." We're talking about the activity that is being generated within the Mind, all between the emotional states all the way up to "4"—what we call the "Master Control Center." So, that is a basic description of what the Standard Model is when we classify it from what is presented in "*The Tablets of Destiny*" material.

We have the Physical Body; we have a Reactive Control Center that governs the emotions; we have a range of thought; and then we have a Master Control Center that basically governs the experience of thought—or the domain or parameters or, basically, the limit or range of what is considered the "Mind-System" as attached to a Human Condition *interior* to a beta-existence.

The other thing that we can demonstrate with this ZU-line —or any kind of gradient scale along it, when we're referring to the Standard Model or distances or the experience of such—is that basically, you have two ends of a spectrum or a gradient scale. For example, when we refer to "0" as "*body-death*," we might consider "8" as "*Infinite Immortality*." That's just one example you could put on there. Another one would be, for example, a "Perfect Knowingness" versus a "Complete Unknown" or a "Complete Mystery" and so forth.

What we do, is we consider these points as *Actualized Awareness*—so, this scale, as an individual can chart themselves higher and higher up the scale on the Standard Model, we're talking about an increase in *Actualized Awareness*; an increase in their ability to take command over the functions of, for example, the Mind-Systems or the Reactive Control Center—they actually undo the patterns of thought or reactive mechanisms that *inhibit* the Self from having a *true* Self-Determined experience with the Human Condition.

I mean, there's nothing *wrong* with deciding to occupy and command a Human Condition to have an experience in this existence. The fact that we've been *entrapped* into one with no further considerations for how we got here and how to get *out* of one—and the fact that these considerations seem to only cause more and more experience of fragmentation and more and more lower level of considerations of what is possible or real—these are the things that make it a *trap*.

Although we've been pointing out "traps" and "pitfalls" along the way in the Mardukite Master Course—when we're talking about Systemology, when we're talking about the relay of it, I mean, really the *trapping* here would be simply just not being able to get out of it; that an individual is working out of their reactive levels and starts becoming so concerned with the Mind-Systems that they never really get past it to the "Spirit"—I guess that would be *one* level of limitation, if there would be one.

But, really, since we've already been able to demonstrate at the Systemology Society or the Mardukite Academy that we're able to push *forward*, and we're able to take the work from Grade-III and actually push forward into Grade-IV.

We already have set up for release, this book called, "*Metahuman Destinations: Piloting the Course to Homo Novus.*" And it's the primary textbook—as much as "*The Tablets of Destiny*" is the core textbook or the introduction, the whole basis, of Grade-III, we've already developed the companion to that.

We're calling it "*Liber-Two.*" It's essentially the basis and formation and evolution of *using* the material that we're covering in Grade-III, as a practical "Piloted" exercise or application of "spiritual advisement," "ministering" and "counseling" individuals to get to higher levels of *Actualized Awareness*.

So, it's not to make it seem boring that: "Oh, we're only dealing at an 'Instructive' level here in the Mardukite Master Course and we're not dealing with 'piloting.'" But, we *are* dealing with the "Core" of it. We're dealing with everything that makes that functional—and honestly [*laughs*] we may just end up making some of these courses or lectures or recordings a *required* part of our Pilot Training Program when we get to that point. Because we're not side-stepping anything.

All of the theory behind it—although there's many practical

applications—"*Crystal Clear*" was designed as a "*self-processing*" manual based on some workshops that I was developing at the inception of Mardukite Systemology in Denver (Colorado) before moving the offices to the San Luis Valley —we were developing all this originally a year ago when we had a small convocation in August that year with some members of the Mardukite Alumni—and some of the founding members of the Systemology Society—in working out a relay in our conference to how to best deliver this material. And that's what "*The Tablets of Destiny*" actually resulted from.

Another way in which the (Standard) Model was divided when we overlaid the ZU-line on top of the *cosmological* Standard Model, was that you were dealing with "physical systems" between 0 and 2; and "thought systems" between 2 and 4; and then everything beyond "4" was just treated as "spiritual systems."

We were eventually able to start elevating—well, more specifics as far as what all of each zone or what each "number" represented—more classifications that began in "*Crystal Clear*." But really we had to—because of how much we had worked at Systemology for nearly a decade, and many of the Alumni from the Grade-II Mardukite Chamberlains work actually weren't really sure how to work or effectively understand any kind of higher application at the time, I had to make *very* certain that "*The Tablets of Destiny*" as a core textbook...

I mean, *this* is the textbook of the Master Course—this "*Systemology Handbook*"—but, "*The Tablets of Destiny*" was the core textbook of the Grade-III development of Mardukite Systemology as an *evolution* of the Mardukite Chamberlains work. As a result of that, we wanted to make absolutely sure that each aspect, whether it was defining the semantics— even defining the semantics *of* the word "semantics"—we wanted to make sure that every point, every "I" was dotted, every "T" was crossed, in making sure that we had a perfected knowledge and a perfected understanding of the Standard Model; and a delivery of it that could actually be applicable or effectively workable as a "Spiritual Tech" to be able to get to higher points of *Actualized Awareness*; not just treat this as a passive philosophy.

When we consider "barriers," "restrictions" and "filters"—and we can demonstrate that, for example, on a ZU-line or in consideration of quantifying, as we do in *"Crystal Clear,"* the various emotional and mental states that an individual is experiencing, it just becomes readily apparent that they do not *actualize* an *Awareness* of *Self* past the point not understood—and this is one of the reasons why we've really on delivered this material at a "Master level" and then are instructing you within the Master Course to deliver, because... this...

Look, as much as an individual can get lost along the way—or confused—concerning the applications or the theory behind, like "Grade-I Magick and Mysticism" or even the history and natures of Mesopotamia and Anunnaki, Grade-III Systemology work is one where if an individual isn't being assisted by a mentor or pilot or instructor in the "academic knowledge lecture" aspects of it, that they could easily fall behind and not reach these new states of *Knowingness*, because there's just too much fragmented data that is getting in the way; or too many imprints and so forth.

A lot of that is treated more practically, even within Grade-III, in the *"Crystal Clear"* text; but, the whole theory—the whole idea—behind why it's practical, why it's functional, the inner workings why the material *in "Crystal Clear" does* deliver the goals that we were pushing for Grade-III. But, the history, development and vocabulary is introduced in *"The Tablets of Destiny"* book.

In some respects, the three principle systems or conditions that we see—whether we're talking about the "physical systems," which are mostly automatic and reactive. They're directly connecting the "emotional" via "biochemical activity" that governs the actual "motor functions." Often times this is where the behavior or the action is triggered, sometimes outside the Self-Determinism of the Alpha-Spirit.

And then we also have the "psychological" or the "Mind-Systems" that is connecting the degrees of thought to the emotional ranges of the "body" and all of this being overseen by "spiritual systems." And so, we can classify this. It's fairly easy to do—to classify it in such a way. You could even classify it as four basic states, if you consider it: spiritual; the Mind-System; emotional; and then the physical body.

But any way you look at that, the three primary systems kind of correlate with the principles of manifestation. And these we see evident in the "Hermetic Philosophy" and the "Arcane Tablets"; but they are: *Consciousness*, *Motion* and *Matter*. That's the way it's relayed in Hermetic Philosophy. And then states of Self-Determinism are: *Beingness*, *Doing* and *Having*. You start to see those crop up in the Model.

The *higher* "up" an individual *is* operating from or the *Actualized Awareness* on the Model, the more at *Cause* they are; and of course, the lower they are on this Model, the more at *Effect* they are.

And of course, the goal here being to get an individual at *Cause* to the highest point possible as *Actualized Awareness*—all the way reaching towards, like I say, all the way to Infinity; we're reaching for the Actualization of Self.

If we put "Infinity" at "8" on the Standard Model and we refer to "Self" as the Alpha-Spirit in the "spirit domain" that is immediately individuated from that at "7." So, we're setting our sights on Infinity—really, in the end, when you consider all of the possible gradients that the work in the future could be—we're setting our sights on *Infinity* so that we can actually *reach* actualization at "7." You know: shoot for 8; hit 7.

And I would say that a complete Self-Actualized independent individuated Alpha-Spirit that is not confined or restricted to any manner of beta-existence, would be pretty much the pinnacle of anything you could possibly do within this lifetime sharing the Human Experience.

So, this might seem a little bit far reaching, but again, all the way up to this point—I mean, we're reaching a point here where an individual that is properly applying at least the Grade-III level of Systemology—that's given in our "*Systemology Handbook*" and our Master Course—honestly, an individual that's *actually* applying this effectively, at the very least, is reaching a point where they're not getting any worse as a Human Condition; not getting any worse as far as their considerations and their point-of-views.

Even if we haven't completely blown out of this universe by the end of Grade-III, what we have found—and this is something that, you know, far surpasses any of the results that we found with lower gradients—but, what we have found is that an individual really just, at the very least, not gonna get any worse.

Now, whether or not they decide to pursue this *beyond* the type of material given in "*The Systemology Handbook*," or whether or not an individual, for example, working through the Mardukite Master Course is going to actually decide to pursue the *higher* levels beyond Grade-III, what we know is at Grade-III we have at *least* achieved a point where an individual is *far* better off than they have ever been in this lifetime.

We can also demonstrate (with) the Standard Model that all thought activity—thought waves, whether fragmented or clear—basically fall between the two points, if we're talking about the Human Condition, the Human Experience; we're not talking about Alpha-Thought—we deal with that at other points along the way.

But, we're talking about a range of activity between the Self-Honest state of, at least, the proactive Mind—the beta-defragmented proactive Mind—as the Master Control Center, which is responsible for directing, for example, the Self-Determinism of the I—the I-AM—toward the "genetic organism" commanding the "genetic vehicle." That would be at "4" on the Standard Model.

The realm of thought exists between 4 and 2; and at "2" you have the Reactive Control Center, which—it basically discharges emotional chemicals to get the "body" to move or do different things; but it actually is almost a "mini-Mind" of itself, it's just only a reactive one—and it can be subject to *imprinting* and *emotional encoding* and so forth.

And so, the thoughts are traditionally meant to direct—traditionally, when you got a clear channel going there, you got the "Mind-Systems" directing the body by using the biochemicals, basically, to get the motor functions to work. The fact that an individual can, you know, be *emotionally charged* or suddenly "angered" by their environment or some other kind of encoding can kick up automatically, this is a point of fragmentation.

An individual, you know, can certainly *choose* to experience whatever emotion they want, but the fact that these can be triggered reactively, we can judge that those levels of *Beingness*—because, if an individual is operating in those states, it's clear that they're not operating full control *over* that thought activity; the thought activity is being influenced or filtered or overshadowed or being, basically, out of commission, in terms of control of the "genetic being"—control over the "body"—by basically letting these emotions determine the mental state, in the absence of *Actualized Awareness*.

So, in situations of *pain* and *loss* and extreme *trauma* and so forth, the Mind is basically eliminated from the equation; the Mind Control Center—the Master Control Center of the

Mind—all thought activity is eliminated and you're dealing with emotional chemicals, you're dealing with the "fight-flight" responses, you're dealing with any kind of activity that is basically just governing the "genetic vehicle."

And this is not always in the best interest of Self—it's simply programmed patterned behavior that is meant to, basically, protect the "genetic vehicle." And it's rarely rational—although it's systematic and programmed, again, it doesn't necessarily serve the logics of analytical thinking; it's just kind of this reactive "reach and withdraw" or "survive and succumb"—or "flinching"—division line.

In most places, they refer to it as the "fight-or-flight" mechanism—as far as "psychology" is concerned—but, in Systemology we know that there is a lot more going on there; imprinting and encoding—certain channels that have been given certain associative knowledge, which is then triggered to produce the results that are, again, outside the Self-Determinism of an individual.

So, if an individual *could be* themselves and *could think* for themselves and *could feel* as they *chose* to—well, we'd have no issues with that. And it's funny, because usually the individual when they are *not* in command of those things, they are usually crying out [*laughs*] about how much they *are.*

: LECTURE 41—THE SYSTEMOLOGY HANDBOOK :
(September 29, 2020)

[*Welcome back to the Academy this morning. This is the forty-first lecture of the Mardukite Master Course. September 29, 2020. And we're at a juncture now where actually—this is actually the "extended course"—the "extended" lectures of the Mardukite Master Course. As you know, originally, we had scheduled forty lectures for the Mardukite Master Course—and although we were able to extend it and still work within the same period of time. Obviously, you know, we had some pretty extensive days last week, getting through the materials of Grade-I and Grade-II. Yesterday, we bridged—we transitioned—between Grade-II "The Route of Mesopotamia" and Grade-III "Mardukite Systemology."*]

And, of course, we were using the context of "*The Tablets of Destiny*" and the release of that—"Liber-One" of Mardukite Systemology, "*The Tablets of Destiny*"—as a transition point; and then also covering "*The Original Thesis*"—portions of "*The Original Thesis*"—which was developed a decade ago and was applied extensively to the Grade-II work and the cuneiform tablets—Arcane Tablets—of Mesopotamia, in order to arrive at the Standard Model.

Had I gone with the original schedule, pretty much that's all we would really have had time to discuss concerning Grade-III Mardukite Systemology; and this is really the first time I'm delivering any lectures—aside from the workshops connected to the book releases and the developments that are taking place—this is the only time I've ever really treated this subject of Mardukite Systemology officially outside of the texts.

In the interim of, essentially, establishing the Master Course —the "Master Grades" —Grades I, II and III and at an "Instructive" level, the Mardukite Masters, which are able to instruct in the material the outer core; basically, the publications and more readily available materials over the last twenty-five years—and be able to deliver, with some significance and (the) duplication factor being taken in account, the extreme amount of material that we have.

Spanning through four Master Edition hardcover anthology releases this year from The Joshua Free Imprint, we're dealing with 3,600 pages of material developed from out of over *thirty* different individual releases that were developed over a quarter-of-a-century. So, a particularly *phenomenal* scope of work that we've been endeavoring to basically attain a Mastery of, within a short period of time—within, essentially, about twenty-four lecture hours catching you up on twenty-four years, you know, of research and discovery; and everything I've been doing, both the surface material and some of this underground background information.

So, what we have now as your Grade-III textbook for the Mardukite Master Course is the Master Edition of the Grade-III material: the textbook *"Systemology Handbook"*—comparable (to), and yet developed at a fraction of the time as any of the other textbooks. Here we have another 800-page textbook, comparable to, for example, *"Merlyn's Complete Book of Druidism"* or *"The Great Magickal Arcanum"* or *"Necronomicon: The Complete Anunnaki Legacy."*

In this essence, we've been able to take the fragments of all of the elements of Systemology, the discourses, the various essays, all the various research and everything that was developed in the last decade (behind-the-scenes)—which honestly, in comparison to what's been (finally) developed in the last year, will be seen as relatively small. But, we had a strong premise to work from and was eventually able to establish, again, the material for Grade-III Mardukite Systemology.

We didn't take it lightly in the consideration that: once I had established what Grade-III would be—the kinda "cut-off" point of materials, the goals having been obtained in those materials and so forth—this wasn't done with *impunity*, this was specifically engineered to reach a specific target. And it was actually able to be accomplished in a relatively short period of time.

We, again, did not take lightly the fact that once we were going to release a *"Systemology Handbook"*—something of that caliber and title and representation, you know, that's something we were kinda gonna be stuck with.

So, really, some very careful attention was given to the idea that the Grade-III material was going to be an extension of everything we had done prior, and that *"The Systemology Handbook"*—the materials within *"The Systemology Handbook"*—was going to be, essentially...

You know, if we didn't hit the target right with this material at this point, there was little hope that we were going to be able to actually extend a practical "Spiritual Tech" or any kind of useful effective workable philosophy behind, for example, "Mardukite Zuism" or any of our—the idea that we were actually going to achieve these goals that had been set forth concerning, for example: the *"Ladder of Lights"* or the *"Pathway to Self-Honesty"*

Fortunately, I can actually stand behind—fully—the work *of* Grade-III, in delivering the exact goals, for example, concerning the Ishtar Gate—concerning Grade-III or the *Third Gate*—concerning emotional reactivity; retaining or returning a greater command and control of the individual back to *Self*, rather than all of the mechanisms and other filters and so forth that are used.

And we had been talking about these concepts for over a decade. However, it's really only been (relatively) recently, that we've been able to accomplish any of the goals on an effective *duplicatable* level; a way that we could actually develop the text for *"The Tablets of Destiny"* and *"Crystal Clear"* to actually reach the points that I've been actually trying to reach for like a decade with this work behind-the-scenes.

And, you know, I had been attacked in all various manners for: using Mesopotamia directly verbatim; going into various aspects of "New Thought"; going into apply ceremonial magic—even five years ago when the Mardukite Alumni and Systemology Society got together and did the "Mardukite Vampyre Academy" for *Moroii ad Vitam* and we developed "*The Vampyre's Handbook*" (materials) at that time. These were all, essentially, efforts to reach the point that we've now been able to reach with Grade-III "Mardukite Systemology" and *beyond*.

So, I thought it would be important if we went through the material—just as far as *what* is contained within "*The Systemology Handbook*" just real briefly. Because, honestly, when you consider the fact that: although Systemology was in, you know, the making for what, over a decade, really most of the material that's contained within this "*Systemology Handbook*" has only been publicly available for about a year now.

As I said: this final grade of material came together rather quickly—and we're actually more than halfway through our developments of Grade-IV already at the Systemology Society; the first portion of that grade already released as "*Metahuman Destinations: Piloting the Course to Homo Novus.*" So, we've actually already established *a step beyond* what the "Mardukite Master Course" contains.

However, as you've experienced over the course *of the last week and a half*, there is a considerable amount of material contained *within* the "Mardukite Master Course" just at an "Instructive" level; just concerning the knowledge grades, the research, the development of everything we're now doing—concerning "Mardukite Zuism" as a religious division; and then the "Systemology Society" as an applied spiritual technology division.

We have definitely already achieved the points of stability concerning these primary grades—these fundamental grades—*one*, *two* and *three*, which are "Instructive" grades, dealing with the last *6,000* years of esoteric knowledge, spiritual traditions, concepts, all various manners of philosophy; which is basically culminated to the point that we're at now with our Systemology.

Even when one is—takes into the count just even the amount of time most of these materials have been around—even most of you *here present*, and many that have already started taking up the Mardukite Master Course from within our own ranks; well, we've had at least a decade, you know, depending on your time of engagement that you've seen the "*Arcanum*" and "*Druid*" materials—and even "*Necronomicon: The Anunnaki Bible*"—is now a decade running.

And so, when it comes to reference or familiarity or certainty—and knowing the material—obviously, *anyone* at any level, regardless of when you've "joined up" or became involved or first began studying or pursuing the Mardukite brand on your own; obviously not have had as much time to get familiar with or be aware of. Most of the individuals now that are looking into our Systemology and looking at our materials that are now being developed and published, this is only the first time that they've even been aware of, for example, the materials of "*The Original Thesis*" or that, you know, there *were* publications—for example, the "Reality Engineering" lectures that were, again, given almost a decade ago.

These concepts we were developing kinda capped off the work about the [*Complete*] "*Anunnaki Bible*" and "*Liber-50*"—"*Sumerian Religion*"—the Anunnaki work that went with that, "*The Complete Book of Marduk by Nabu*" and "*Necronomicon Revelations*" as "*Liber-R*"—all of that was completed in 2010. So, by 2011, I was pretty much "ready-set-go" [*laughs*] to begin the Systemology Society and actually, you know, move people on to the next point.

And it really *did* require another decade of underground development to reach this point, but we've been able to hit—we've been able to hit the mark that I've originally wanted to accomplish since the 1990's and the development of a program of "Beta-Defragmentation." And this is, again, something I've been working at on my own for now over two decades—and this was accomplished, again, with the Grade-III work of Mardukite Systemology; the release of the fundamentals and theory behind it being released as "*The Tablets of Destiny*" and then, the practical handbook or "self-processing" manual that was released as "*Crystal Clear*."

Of course, both of those materials—the materials for both those books—"*Tablets of Destiny*" and "*Crystal Clear*" appear in this "*Systemology Handbook.*" And, of course, yet again, I was mentioning *yesterday*, that it also has the introduction —"*Mardukite Zuism: A Brief Introduction*"—as the premise, which we covered yesterday, actually.

And it includes the "Introductions"—the "Forewords"—by Reed Penn, which it was originally one essay, and I decided to break it into two parts; and so, the first part was actually the foreword to the original release of "*The Tablets of Destiny*" and then the second part was actually used as the "Introduction" when we published the transcripts to "*The Power of Zu*" lectures, which I gave publicly last year—I believe at the very end of December—and the transcripts to those appear not only the "appendix" to "*The Systemology Handbook,*" but also your "Instructor's Manual" for the Mardukite Master Course.

To be honest, I'm mostly just happy we were able to maintain an underground following of the Systemology Society, even though it wasn't publicly visible—it was in a developmental stage longer than what one might expect and still have something come to fruition; because, most endeavors would have collapsed by that time.

Although it ["*The Original Thesis*"] wasn't enough for us to *really* launch any kind of publicly visible, you know, "brand" under the Mardukite umbrella concerning the "applications," there really—it was really, at the time of "*The Original Thesis*" nearly a decade ago, it was really primarily theory. It was... not that it *wasn't* workable or wasn't effective or didn't "ring true" and make sense—that's one of the things that kinda kept those *along* with it for so long, even though there really was very little added to it.

After the contributions of "*The Original Thesis*," which incidentally are also collected—we has to kinda make sure we were careful about how we were delivering stuff, because although we don't really use it as a basis for our Systemology anymore; we prefer to introduce people to it through "Mardukite Zuism" or with "*The Tablets of Destiny*" or "*Crystal Clear*"—but, "*The Original Thesis*" composed of several booklets that I was mentioning yesterday, like "*Human, More Than Human*," "*Defragmentation*," "*Trans-Human Generations*," "*Systemology for Life: Patterns and Cycles*"—these are all collected in the appendix of "*The Systemology Handbook*" with a very specific editor's note and introduction that this is basically being maintained for posterity.

I mean, at this juncture, we're treating *every single piece* of information regarding the development of Systemology, when we talk about Grade-III and a Grade-III textbook, "*The Systemology Handbook.*" Although, as I say, some of this becomes—at the point an individual... if you've already worked through "*The Tablets of Destiny*" or "*Crystal Clear*," this kind of becomes a little bit redundant; *or*, it could be used as really good review.

These were really—they were such monumental writings, as brief as it was, that it captivated many individuals that had already worked through the "Mardukite Core" by 2010-2011 while we were doing it. Others now, obviously just finding this stuff or just discovering our work or those that you encounter that are still new to our brand, well, yeah, there seems to be a lot to catch up on—but this is taking into account that I've spent a quarter-of-a-century developing this for the explicit purpose and the intention that it would take another individual a quarter-of-a-century of their lifetime to get through this.

In a *week and a half*—of course, we've blown through it with the idea that you have a lot of reference material at your disposal and background already in the Mardukite tradition —but, in the last *week and a half*, we've been able to cover more ground than even most, just, standard texts or standard ideas that are put forth as a tradition or system or various encyclopedias of "magick" or "mysticism" you might get.

Of course, we're encompassing multiple books when we're doing this—it's not to say this is all one... But, at the same time, let us consider that if we... well, *when we* release transcripts of the lectures as a publication, *that* publication in and of itself, and everything that's been covered as a dialogue—not even including everything you can go in and reference with what we have in our materials—but just what we have discussed and covered as lectures in the last *week and a half*, well, this is a pretty monumental staple or turning point or apex when it comes to the state of knowledge—the state of Knowingness—and the current state of the Human Condition and where we're reaching.

Because, *now* we're getting an individual—at Grade-III— we're getting an individual, as I said *yesterday*, kind of up to a point of "*zero.*" We're trying to get them back to just a point of, essentially, like a "clean slate" on which, yeah, there's plenty of stuff you can develop.

There's a lot of ideas behind "defragmentation," where an individual has the sense that they're "losing something"; that all of this stuff that they're carrying around with them *is* something to "have." So, this can be, you know, remedied with the *proper* applications of "*systemologic processing*"—but at the same time, you're dealing with getting an individual back to a point where they can actually *live* their life, at the very least, when you're talking about Grade-III and the Master-level of "Instruction."

All of this that I refer to when we're talking about Seekers, when we're talking about the work that's done—when we're talking about instructing and mentoring—all of this just as readily applies to *you*; *you* as the individual; *you* as a Master. I mean this is a Master-level of instruction intended for *you*.

But, the purpose behind becoming and the way to play the game when it comes to society, when it concerns physical existence, when it concerns what we're doing when we reach *beyond* just ourselves and we're reaching beyond to those Spheres of Influence *beyond* our "Self" and our "Home" and even our immediate "groups" as we're trying to create a change—a shift in consciousness—*in* what it means to *be* "Human" and the "Human Condition."

And by that, we're talking about *all* of Humanity, in one respect or another. Whether or not we can actually *reach* every single—of all the billions of people—that's not what we mean. There's the idea of a "tipping point." There's the idea of the 99th monkey—I'm not gonna get into that; you can look into that. The idea, though, that basically once there is enough of a shift taking place with enough individuals interacting with the "Spheres" *within* their reach—each of those individuals—well, then now we can create a better world; we can create change.

There's this idea that unless we reach every single individual that we can't create the changes we want to see on the planet—that's just ridiculous. It really just takes *one* properly Self-Determined tenacious individual to create some pretty incredible changes on *this* planet.

We're dealing with a nuts and bolts "billiard ball" Physical Universe *down here*, being commanded by a *very powerful* and *very wise—very intelligent*, if you want to apply that; because we're talking about the Alpha-Spirit—we're talking about something that essentially, you know, "close to godliness" is about as omniscient and omnipresent and so forth as what we've always attributed to some *outside* Source.

So, when we consider what the true capabilities—the creative faculties—of the Self *is*, when it can actually be freed up and actualized enough to have that kind of command and reach and authority *over* this Human experience, there really is no saying *what* an individual can do.

And by this, I'm not trying to impose some "crazy, supernatural, metaphysical" application of "super-powers" here; we're talking about the *basic* things that people do every day—the basic things within their Sphere of Influence. And then by achieving the great things within those Spheres of Influence, having the *certainty* and the *reach* and the *willingness* to go into greater and greater Spheres of Influence and create these changes and actually affect the Universe the way that all of these "magical traditions" and "religious philosophies" and various cultural "priesthoods" and "(secret) societies" have been claiming to do, you know, for 6,000 years.

So, you know, it's kind of like: "time to put the money where your mouth is" so-to-speak, when we're talking about a "Master-level" of understanding; because, we're talking about a level of understanding and knowledge now, which carries a *huge* amount of "responsibility" *and equally* a huge amount of "power"—and those two go together.

And this is what it means to be a "Master"—a "Master of this Universe."

Now then, the text copy of the original—it looks like April 30, 2011—there was a special announcement about the "NexGen Systemological Society" being founded. And this was issued to the "Mardukite Chamberlains" explaining that: "We have formed and established a new division for

Alumni that is dedicated to a new avenue of spiritual and scientific pursuits—one that will increase understanding of the Human Condition as experienced by modern man. Further, it directly affects the future of the *next generation* of Human and the future of the planet."

"Who are you? Where do you come from? Where are you going? What is reality? Why do you feel and think as you do? Does this experience come from Self—or, does it stem from artificial programming? What does all this even mean and how can Self-Actualization even be achieved in this Lifetime?"

"On the brink of a new chapter for Humanity, it's time we addressed these questions with a new true Self-Honest *NexGen* paradigm—one that provides real answers so startling clear that they point toward a new evolution of consciousness, the reality engineering and piloting of the next evolution of Human experience, or 'trans-human' existence as a spiritual being, free of dependency on external technologies."

Of course, we've actually gotten away from the terminology about "transhumanism." *Transhumanism* (as a subject) has (more recently) come to, essentially, regard the *outer-external* "technological" aspects of what could be used to enhance the Human Condition. It doesn't treat anything about the "Self"—has nothing to do with the Spirit or the Mind—and what it understands as "consciousness" really has to do with "electrical signals" in the "*brain.*"

And so (*now in Transhumanism*) you're talking about "Life Extension" in terms of "cryogenics" or "bionic" additions; you're talking about "Space Migration" because, you know, obviously the Human Condition didn't do very well here, so why not go mess up somewhere else—under this premise that it's easier to, essentially, restart and terraform an "*almost dead*" planet, than to correct issues taking place on this one... This is what boggles me about the Human Condition.

Really, if you consider what we were looking at a decade ago, just in the founding of the Systemological Society, it basically, again, it took a decade, and the culmination of all the materials now found within "*The Systemology Handbook*," in order to achieve these effective results (in our work).

When we talk about the ability of an individual to actually change the shape of "consciousness"—not only their own consciousness, but the state of the world—one of the places where I've found this to be incredibly effective, or taking place so-to-speak, was the West Coast.

So, what ended up happening—and I've never really made too much of a personal account regarding a lot of the underground explorations that I've been a part of. The irony is that at the time of completing the Mardukite Core and launching the Systemology Society in 2011, I had pretty much reached what I was considering the pinnacle or the end-point on the development *of* the "Mardukite" system and was moving forward.

I had also just had a "systemological" *slash* "Druidic" writing published in Douglas Monroe's final volume of the "Merlyn Trilogy" called "*The Deepteachings of Merlyn*." And I figured I was pretty much on my way to the next point—and yet all through 2011, the *swell* of the "Systemology" work just was *not happening*; it was still essentially these few booklets and notes that were *hinting* toward something, but not delivering *per se*. And I wasn't in a position, at that time, to *take it* any further.

By the end of 2011, I was actually beginning what became a *five-year* journey of... well, "*journeying*"—traveling around, essentially the West Coast to the East Coast, from the upper points of the Pacific Northwest to all the way down to Key West, the most southern and eastern point in the United States. I spent a lot of time traveling; staying in a lot of different places; doing mentorships; doing research.

There weren't a lot of new publications taking place during that time. I was, basically, working on the backbone of Systemology—still developing this outer work, or this greater work, while maintaining the outer work; for example, the work concerning the Wizard Schools and maintaining the publication of "*Arcanum*" and the "*Anunnaki Bible*" and so forth; maintaining, essentially, the Mardukite Chamberlains while trying to build up some *steam* [*laughs*] for this Systemology.

And so, one of the places I spent a considerable amount of time, was California—particularly, I guess it would be Southern California and also San Francisco, which some people consider Southern California—it's really more central. When I considered the fact that the Rosicrucians, or the O.T.O., or the Hermetic Order of Lux, or Theosophical, the New Orders and Reformed Orders of the Golden Dawn, Anton LaVey's Church of Satan, the Temple of Set—I mean, even the Church of Scientology and the Bohemian Grove... These had all been basically been operating within a particular area in the United States, which was San Francisco, if not Los Angeles.

So, I spent a lot of time in these areas—and I spent it underground, dealing with a caliber of society that some individuals, probably, don't even like to face exists in this world. But, more to the point, I was able to, basically, practice not only the skills of what I had already learned of concerning "magick" and "spiritualism" and "mysticism" and all that; but also, really the advanced work of Systemology—the work that I'm actually *getting back to* now at this point.

And one of the interesting things that was taking place in the underground—particularly in San Francisco; I imagine it was happening in other places to and continues to in the United States, but—my experiences being in San Francisco, and it was called "The Games" or the "Magic Games."

I did write a booklet—I did write a short discourse regarding some of that; nothing too revealing—but I did release it in the same series as *"The Original Thesis"* booklets, and so the material for that is actually contained in the appendix of *"The Systemology Handbook."*

So, there is a discourse called *"The Games,"* which actually very few people know about. But, it was kind of an experience. And just to give a brief summary of it. The idea being —because, we've been talking a lot about emotional reactivity, response mechanisms, programming and so forth.

When you're playing "The Games"—or the "Magic Games"— the idea being that you're basically operating in *extremes*; you're operating in extreme conditions, whether they be physical or spiritual—and you're basically testing yourself; you're basically seeing what you're *going to do*; you're seeing what you're *able to do*; you're seeing what your skills are.

And this is primarily an individual effort, although there's enough people doing it that it seems that, you know, it overlaps—people are doing things in different areas or they're doing things onto each other. But, it has to do with, basically, being able to maintain yourself: can you maintain your Self—can you maintain who you are? Have you even found who you are?—while, basically, pitting yourself up against all the various "elements"; all the various "things" you can "imagine."

It's difficult to really put into words... An individual that has had a handling of "magick" and "mysticism"—that has worked with various spiritual energies—that's familiar with the way that different godforms and archetypes are manifested, depending on how you're dealing with them—the Anunnaki or some other cultural mythology.

Those that had been delving into Systemology—looking at the processing and the way the function of the Mind works; the command of the Mind-Body connection by the Alpha-

Spirit—some of this really just actually comes into "play" or comes into "place"; because, what's happening is you're taking everything that you "know" and simply applying it. And of course, in these conditions you're not...

This was a situation where I didn't have a fixed schedule. There was nobody waiting on me—I didn't have any responsibilities; I wasn't responsible for anyone and no one was responsible for me. And it was a way of actually demonstrating to myself, with certainty, that—what was true was true and what wasn't, wasn't.

Really, if you start working with this stuff to any great extent, you're going to have some experiences—and you're probably going to have some phenomenon. And that's all fine and good. There's really no reason to *risk the invalidation* of it—there's no point in talking about it. Those that are going to achieve certain points of realization will simply be in that state of *Knowing* at each one of these states, and we've been able to grade that—not only within the "Knowledge Lectures" or the "Knowledge Grades" or in terms of the type of information accumulated, but we've been able to grade that, using for example, the Standard Model, the ZU-line, the idea of "Actualized Awareness" in actually determining where somebody actually falls within that—and by that understanding being able to have a greater control over one's own "Actualized Awareness."

: LECTURE 42—MASTER CONTROL :
(September 29, 2020)

In yesterday's lecture on *"The Original Thesis,"* I covered the portion of that text where I describe the "Matrix-System"—the "Matrix of Light"—the idea that the Matrix is, essentially, a "field" of *potentiality*. And that's what we consider the ALL—All Existence—the "Potential Everythingness" that contrasts the "Infinity of Nothingness" and the opposing, balancing, factor; without which there is no existence—there is no motion.

Now, of course, to have an (scientific) field called "Systemology," we have to take up, frequently, with the study—and the concepts associated with the study—of *"systems."* And the difference being—and why we differentiate it as "Mardukite Systemology" or "NexGen Systemology" and in advanced levels, even "Metahuman Systemology"—is that this idea of a "study of systems" is actually *not* unique to me and *not* something that I've personally developed from "scratch."

The idea and pursuit of "Systems," "Cycles" and "Patterns"; "cycles" and "patterns" pretty much constituting *what* a "Dynamic System"—*"dynamic"* being something that changes, that is changing facets or factors—that a "Dynamic System" *has*. This has been the exploration of natural philosophies and spiritual philosophies and applied spiritual technologies for thousands of years. This is—this is *old stuff.*

And we've been basically reviving the "cream of the crop" of it; we've been "cherry picking" the best of it—the most workable methods—putting it on a gradient scale of reach and basically plotting out particular goals, using systematic logic to achieve, basically, each tier that represents—we've covered the symbolism behind the sevenfold Gate system—

what each tier represents. By doing this systematically, we've been able to achieve the results.

I don't know how far this extends out to. Obviously the goal being: *"Gateways to Infinity"*—but by progressing in a very logical manner and observing patterns, cycles, and applying our systematic knowledge to ancient wisdom and using it to actually find applicable effective ways of *doing something* and achieving the goals.

This is what *defines* our Systemology—our "Mardukite Systemology"—because you will find in other pursuits or in supplemental research or anything that you might go and look for at a more academic level, that the idea of "Systemology"—or more specifically *"systemotology"*—has been a field, basically, a field divided from advanced mathematics or theoretical mathematics and game theorists and what not, at an academic university level for a hundred years.

So, the idea behind "Systems Theory" is actually very old; even at an academic level. And then, if we consider ancient philosophies—well, "Systems Theory" is really at the heart of *all* pursuits concerning "knowledge" and the "Human Condition."

We know that, really, everything that exists, does so, based on "patterns," which are operating at various levels and degrees of observation. And when they are observed over time—when you're seeing changes in *space-over-time*—this is observed by, essentially, a "calculative," you know, "mathematically logical analytical mind"; and then it's *that* significance that's given to it—that's what gives the significance of whatever the magnitude or degree is in the measured intervals—the phases—whatever is compared, in terms of "masses" compared to other "masses."

We say, you know, "time" is *relative*; well, relative does not mean "non-existent." And "time" is given a significance by the Observer; but the idea that it's an illusion is a direct contradiction to the idea that we *can* observe "cycles." And within the idea that there's a certain "ebb and flow" of these cycles, you can find that there is a systematic logic behind their appearances and, you know, as is found, for example, (in) any type of "programming" or "encoding." And this is what we call the pattern.

So, when you combine "cycles" and "patterns" you have "*systems.*"

And if you consider the most—at the most practical level—when you consider "cycles" and "patterns," you could consider, for example, "behavioral systems" in an individual—the ones that are essentially programmed as "personality"—I mean, these can be evaluated on these terms, and this is why I say, a lot of this runs halfway in the field of metaphysics and the other half running, you know, along the side of psychology in many respects.

But, we're dealing—this is just *one* physical example—we're dealing with all kinds of work when we're talking about Systemology; but that the same concepts—the same systematization of knowledge—can be applied to human behavior. It's just that "human behavior" is—the *prediction* of "human behavior"—becomes more of a *byproduct* of this *higher* level understanding, rather than the direct target of its pursuit; and this is where psychology began to falter.

I mean, my original academic pursuits were, for example, even in "psychology" and I cover some of that background and my experiences and what kind of led to the development—my personal development—in to Systemology, and a lot more of those details in "*The Power of Zu*" lectures. And that's why those (transcripts) are included in not only the appendix of "*The Systemology Handbook*," but also your "*Instructor's Manual.*" And that's why I've kinda been careful—I'm trying to not actually even go back over that same information, because those lecture transcripts are right there.

When we talk about "Mardukite Systemology" and "Spiritual Systemology"—or even "Metahuman Systemology"—we're also talking about the application of "Systems Theory" and "Games Theory" and all of this, that you *could treat* strictly at a physical, pragmatic, mundane, material universe level—but we're applying the same principles to *higher* levels. And that's where we're seeing our best results.

And the reason why we explore, for example, this material as "Systemology" or even incorporating "Systems Theory" is because, this is what—when we're talking about "patterns" and "cycles" and "systems"—this is what we directly deal with when we talk about "emotional reactivity," the control of the "genetic vehicle," the command (of) the "Mind-System" free of "fragmentation." I mean, *this* is what we're dealing with.

We're making *assumptions* about our "world" every day; we're looking "out" into the "world" and using, basically, a pre-formatted set of data or knowledge patterns in order to give it any meaning—to make sense of our world. I mean, this is one of the things that differentiates, for example, the experience that a "small child" have in relation to the outer environment, versus someone that's been incarnate as that "genetic vehicle" in this lifetime for countless decades.

I mean, we're talking about the idea that *all objects* are given significances and meaning, classifications and titles, and then *that* is being differentiated and associated with other things—things being "similar or "dissimilar"—and at the very lowest level of understanding, things are either all a certain thing—they're either the same as something or they are not at all the same as something.

This is type of "on-off"—*ones* and *zero*—type reasoning that traditionally, without really being in command of the Human experience, that as time goes on, it really does become more and more "fixed" in terms of the parameters or the range of what any kind of "considerations" are. Because, well: "everything is just what it is and it's all taken for granted and there really is no personal Will or determination or thought or consideration or creativity going into the human experience any more" —the individual is becoming more and more the *effect* of their environment as opposed to the other way around.

And that's another reason why—I mean, even... we talk about the classification and codification of knowledge and its conditioning—or imprinting—on the human experience, when we talk about the incorporation of language and writing in ancient Mesopotamia. And that's one of the key highlights of that Grade-II material, in terms of its *effect* on the Human Condition.

Really, this idea of "classification" and "labels"—it becomes more and more important when we're talking about "communication." That's why we say that, you know, "fragmentation" is almost inherent *in* the Human Condition *in* communication, because we're fixing each other to space and time in these bodies and locating each other there as, you know, cause and effect—or receipt and sending point of communications—we're using *language*, which has been codified and systematized and given all these various *associations* and emotional attributes, given whatever an individual's experiences are; and this is, you know, what we're treating as "*Reality.*"

We look at this more holistically in Systemology, because this is—the defragmentation—is to make this as clear as possible. Even in the deliver of a new science or a new field —or the classification of "Mardukite Systemology" and so forth—we spend a considerable amount of time in Grade-III concerning definitions, vocabulary and semantics; not because we want to be all "*nerdy*" about this and sound all academic and look at our grandiose vocabulary, but we want to make sure that we're not just becoming *another* "field"—another "physical science"—where everything just becomes the most mundane, and based on that.

Our field is based on a progression that almost *precedes* itself. We don't go out there and go: "Well, we haven't been able to make any of this work, but if we were to equate in this *'globbertron'* and, you know, then all these particles that we have would actually make sense; and if we just look hard enough, then we'll probably find one of these suckers." That's traditionally the way that science has been progressing forward [*laughs*] outside of these, you know, "higher" pursuits.

I mean, prior to dealing with the idea of "emotional encoding" and "imprinting" and "mental programming," this idea of patterns—and cycles of them kind of feedbacking on each other and establishing deeper patterns—was expressed right from the beginning in the heart of the inception of Systemology in "*The Original Thesis.*"

"*Patterns and Cycles*" is actually one of the titles—it was called "*Systemology for Life: Patterns and Cycles*"—and it was one of the booklets, one of the discourses that was produced that became part of "*The Original Thesis.*" That information, again, is also in "*The Systemology Handbook*" and in the publication called "*Systemology: The Original Thesis.*"

We've kept it in print for posterity, because there's nothing in it that contradicts any of the work that we're doing now. The work that we're doing now is just operating on a little bit more of a "functional" level in terms of applications and thought exercises—what we refer to as "processing" in Systemology.

But this concept of patterns and cycles actually makes a return in both "*The Tablets of Destiny*" and "*Crystal Clear*" when were referring to, for example, what is classified as the "Figure-8" pattern or like the "infinity loop" that an individual gets themselves into; and we put that up on the Standard Model, where we classify a particular point within the mental range—for example, between "2" and "4"—which seems to have an association or "encoded trigger" that sends an individual down into an emotional range, between 0.1, I guess—or basically just *zero*—and 2.

An individual can actually, after charting the points of Awareness that they are reaching—the connectivity of associated knowledge and emotional encoding—(they) can actually observe these behavior patterns, and looking at it from a higher Systemological perspective than just what you might treat, for example, in psychology or something.

We're looking at "human behavior," but we're looking at the *pattern* of which specific mental states and specific emotional states are correlated and then are treating those. In doing so, we're able to alleviate this kind of "automatic response-mechanism" that an individual carries with them, where they are not in control necessarily of the thought or "Mind-Systems" or so forth, because the Awareness—their point of Beingness and what they are identifying with, you know, the reality that is taking place around them—is basically kind of "sling-shotting" them between these two points at lower levels of "beta-Awareness."

And this is where you also get the idea where an individual —you'll notice individuals—where they keep stumbling on the same point; they keep running into the same obstacles or they keep triggering these same patterns in their life— and just don't seem to understand why. And this is something—if this is treated at a systematic level, it's a lot easier to identify, because *there it is.*

We use the Standard Model and we use classifications of various emotional and mental states—and we're able to clearly identify where an individual is at and actually *make* predictions concerning "human behavior" on that premise, rather than, again, making, you know, prediction and control of human behavior at the most physical and material level our priority—which is what the material sciences and even psychology has done.

And it's almost in direct defiance to its name; because, it's no longer a science of the "Mind," it's a science of "human behavior"—and so, again, we don't really tread into classifying any of our work... I mean, we're dealing with Grade-III "Mardukite Systemology"—a development of "ancient wisdom" that's already been ignored [*laughs*] for thousands of years by academicians; other than the blatant physical literal translation of artifacts.

We're not treading on any other people's "toes" here—and honestly, they don't really have anything to do with our domain; their physical sciences have, basically, only led them to further and further agreements with the conditions of this material universe. They've no longer looked to become anything—or establish a point of *being* anything—outside of the considerations of Human existence, or the Human Condition rather, in beta-existence.

And any kind of upgrade on that, as I said, we've kind of put aside the idea of *"trans-humanism"* and taken up the term *"meta-humanism,"* because transhumanism now represents this idea of using "artificial intelligence" and "cryogenics" and "cybernetics" and "robots" and, you know, various ways of supposedly storing "consciousness" in some "database" or (at) "data centers."

That's not what we're interested in. There's nothing that the individual is going to carry with them out of this lifetime *with that*. There is nothing that the Spirit—which we know is eternal, which we know has existences prior to this and certainly afterward—not of that (transhumanist) focus is going to benefit one any; if anything it's going to hinder, because all we're going to do during the course of this lifetime is to contribute to or continue to validate the lowest level of patterns and cycles that we encounter in this material existence.

Now, in the lectures *yesterday*, I was introducing the Standard Model and the materials from, for example, *"The Tablets of Destiny.*" And in doing so, we discussed, for example, on the Standard Model—I've been saying how we chart thought between, well, "2.1" and "4"; and emotion of the genetic vehicle between "0.1" and "2"—and the reason being is that using our model, at "2" and "4" we've been able to establish the idea of these "relay centers" or "Control Centers."

And so at "4," we're talking about the "Master Control Center"—which is a point of contact between Alpha and Beta existence; the directed ZU-energy as an impulse being sent or an energy flow being sent, directed from the Alpha Spirit toward the Mind-System, which is not the same as "Self." The Self or the Alpha-Spirit *isn't* the "Mind" any more than it's the "Body" or what the *body* is *feeling.*

But the "Master Control Center" is essentially this perfect computing device—well, it's perfect to the extent of the information, of course, that is being received or is being sent to it. And that's why when we chart that, we put the "Master Control Center" at "4" on the Model, which is the division point of the Human Condition as it relates to beta-existence.

We refer to everything between "4" and "0"—and all those possible emotional states and all those states of Mind—as *beta* states. And so, when we talk about "beta-defragmentation," we're talking about, for example, if we consider the physical "continuity" of physical existence of the Physical Universe at "zero," than we are looking at it—or experiencing it—with this "genetic vehicle" at *that* level of contact.

We're talking about the level of physical "inert" matter there—physical *contact*; solid bodies, solid walls. We're using a Mind-System to experience that, which is put here at "4."

Any fragmentation—any kind of *blockages*—any kind of imprinting or filters that are installed, any kind of places where *Awareness* is being "*trapped*"—whether it's somewhere in the "Mind" between "2" and "4" or, you know, all the kind of "debris" that is collected along the way: we call this the *"fragmentation."*

And so, you know, when we refer to the "Master Control Center" as this perfect computing device—well, yeah, because it will accept all of the information that it receives and calculate based on that, from these lower levels of sensory experience and the perceptions, filters, you know—the stuff that is *within* the Human Condition; the range of experience.

Any kind of fragmentation on the line—it's going to send the wrong information; it's going to send *fragmented* information. And so, that's where these concepts and this vocabulary comes from. It's not just arbitrary or fanciful; it's actually very specific, very systematic; and it's been selected with only the greatest care.

And this is why I say: if an individual is stuck with all this misaligned misassociated knowledge at the realm of thought *and* has got all this emotional encoding tied to all these various experiences within the realm of the "Reactive Control Center" *and then*, you know, has all these associated cross-programs that basically keep slinging them between *this* mental state and *this* emotion and just "jamming them up, back and forth"—I don't know how an individual could ever say that they're actually thinking or experience life or reality *in* such a fragmented state.

[*A gap in the original masters occurs here to remove a period of silence and background noise during a question asked by a student, inaudible to the recordings.*]

So, traditionally—I mean, yeah, at higher levels. I mean, at the time, we weren't really sure *how far* this was going to go; particularly when I was establishing *"The Tablets of Destiny."* I was thrilled enough to be doing *"The Tablets of Destiny"* and getting Mardukite Systemology on the road. I didn't expect that, honestly, that *"Crystal Clear"* would be put together in *only two months*, following the publication of "*The Tablets of Destiny.*"

And when you look at the material for that, you can see why that seems incredible—the scope of what we were developing—because, essentially between August and the end of October, I had put together both "*The Tablets of Destiny*" *and* "*Crystal Clear*," which is the main bulk *of* Grade-III Mardukite Systemology.

So, at the time, we were basically just treating *that* as the point of "beta-defragmentation"—basically getting an individual this "crystal clear" line of vision up to the Master Control Center and referring to that as the point of "Self-Honesty." And so, that is why Grade-III, as we were developing it, not really certain where we were going beyond that—because I knew at least having achieved what we did with "*Crystal Clear*," I knew that Grade-III was completed and that the "Master" material, everything that I had been trying to get to at the most fundamental levels since the 1990's, had been achieved.

And hence: the release of the "Master Editions" of *all* the materials—*and* the "Mardukite Master Course."

The "Master Control Center" (at "4") we also refer to as the "MCC"—just to be more concise; and then, at what we plot at "2" on the Standard Model is the "Reactive Control Center" and this is referred to often times as the "RCC." And this is basically a secondary—or reactive—communication system that *is* part of the "Mind-System," but it's inherently attached to the "genetic vehicle."

Whereas the "Mind-System" *proper*, like for example, the "Master Control Center," is a point of contact for the "Mind-System" for the Alpha-Spirit directing it from, well relatively speaking, from "above."

And then the "Mind-System" has another point of contact:

the "Reactive Control Center," which is inherently determined by the conditions and experiences of the "genetic vehicle" or the "physical body" from down "below."

And so, this interconnectivity between the "MCC" and the "RCC" is what we constitute as the "Mind-System." And it's, inherently, it's basically a "feedback loop," which is this complete continuous circuit—flow of energy or information; because we consider these (as) relay points of "information."

For example, when we're talking about specific classifications of an individual, for example, feeling "sadness" or "anger" or "antagonistic" or something—these are specific points that are considered, given those classifications, it's considered "information." When we're treating it at the highest level—when we're just talking about the flows within any systems—we can also be treating this as "energy."

So, we have this "feedback loop," which is inherently a circuit flow of energy or information, and this is—we treat the subject of "communication" a little bit more deeply at higher Grades of Systemology—but we're inherently talking about the basic "return" of information and then the "supply" of information, and this continuous flow, which is essentially "communication."

This circuit or loop is, essentially—when we started looking at this flow, this pattern—these circuits and loops are what we start treating at in Grade-IV "Piloted Systemology" or Metahuman Systemology; we start treating these directly. At the level of, for example, my relay in "*The Tablets of Destiny*," it was enough to be able to observe them and know that they *existed*.

Where the "Master Control Center"—"MCC"—is essentially analytical, functioning on logic patterns, the "Reactive Control Center"—"RCC"—really has to do with encoded automated responses, which you know, again, we're treating "emotions," so we call them "emotionally encoded responses" or "reactive responses" that concern—essentially, they kick in whenever the "genetic vehicle" or the "genetic organism" is considering itself in danger or in threat of loss or so forth.

So, what happens—and, I mean, this is a standard pattern that's learned and then reinforced over time when it's not treated or "defragmented"—but, what happens is: rather than actually having a clear view or experience of whatever is taking place, the "Reactive Control Center" sends signals based on experience and former *imprinting* back to the "Mind-System" that basically says, "I got this. We've dealt with this before and we got through it and this is what's going on and this is how things are gonna be."

This kind of *imprinting* is essentially the deepest of fragmentation that an individual can have; because it basically eliminates an actual Self-determined "command" *of* the Human experience, by allowing all these automated control mechanisms to basically take over.

The "Reactive Control Center" really—it's not that there's anything "wrong" with it *per se*, but it has the ability to operate independently, or to overthrow or short-circuit the upper systems—anything above it—when it's stimulated. And so, when it comes to "command and control" of the Human experience and the Human Condition, well, yeah, having all that fragmentation is something to be concerned about.

So, in that respect we're talking about the states of "Mind" and the "emotional" states, the reactivity, the ability to command the "Master Control Center" we charted on the Standard Model—this is all concerning, basically, *your reality* in beta-existence, in the Physical Universe. And this is the way that we chart it as individuals—the individual states of *Actualized Awareness*. And of course, we could apply the same concepts to "groups" and to "societies" and so forth.

I mean, when we consider: most of our experience, even in beta-existence, when we're concerning like "contact with vibrations" and "matter" and so forth, it's really encounters with the "lifeforms" that we meet—and the most significant being, of course, those in our immediate vicinity; or even authority figures, family, our communities and so forth, you know.

Each of these represent various levels of—and this has been theorized or talked about even in "creative psychology"—a certain "group consciousness" field. And, I mean, it's kind of fed by the thought participation—the thoughts of those that are inherently occupying the "group" or any that are in *agreement* as *reality*.

Because that's what *reality* essentially is: it's what is being *agreed* to.

It doesn't necessarily concern itself with what things *actually* are; just what is considered *real*, what is considered *real* to the individual or their experience. And when we talk about "social programming" or we talk about the "norm" and whatnot, this is of course, affected by those that are sharing the Human Condition and kind of fall into this certain "average" when it comes to what kind of gradient we can plot the level of understanding or *Actualized Awareness* when we're talking about a "group."

Because this is, you know—in order to be in good communication among a group, you pretty much need to share a certain level of agreement and reality, and so this kind of begins to form the basic "consciousness" *of* the "group." And as a result, it basically creates the "standard" and validates whatever position that it's at in its own cycles—just as an individual can have its own programming and imprinting and its own "figure-8" patterns and so forth, you could just as easily observe and apply the same systematic concepts to "groups" and social ordering.

The reason why we push for more of this "Self-Actualization" and "*higher levels* of *Actualized Awareness*"—for example, even the Mardukite Master Course, delivering a Master-level of instruction, to have you be able to duplicate the same—to demonstrate the same—level and degree of understanding that we maintain at the Mardukite Academy *proper*, wherever *you* are in your handling of the Human experience and other individuals that you're treating with this; your Seekers, your apprentices, the students that are coming to your branches of the Academy or temples, lodges, churches, whatever it may be.

Because rather than falling into agreement with the lowest denominator and the common standards, there's also this idea that certain individuals will gravitate towards the higher level or charismatic personalities, which radiate the reality that they're wanting to agree with—those that are looking for something more; those that are aware of... even those that have already worked through the type of material that we deal with at Grade-I and Grade-II, but are still seeking or have already tried other avenues, but have still been gravely disappointed—all of this, it's really up to the individual, your certainty, your charisma, your mastery of this and familiarity with it, that's going to shine forth; that's going to be what others are gonna pick up on—and your personal success, your ability to demonstrate the principles that have been relayed all throughout this course, particularly up into Systemology and so forth, into your own life so that, as an example, you're basically attracting those that are looking to be where you are and to have this type of master-level of all the graded material that we've been dealing with, and also a greater handling over the "Mind-Body" connection and the Human experience.

: LECTURE 43—COMMANDING THE MIND :
(September 29, 2020)

We know our "thoughts" and "personal vibrations"—these frequencies and flows, this energy—it definitely has the ability to affect our experience of reality, what we consider *affecting us*. Unfortunately, you know, the more an individual is experiencing lower and lower considerations—and lower and lower experiences—their Awareness is fixed to lower points, for example, on the beta-Awareness scale that we introduce in *"Crystal Clear"* material; or even in *"The Tablets of Destiny,"* on the Standard Model in general—these become fixed points of "Beingness" and "Awareness" *as* Self.

So, the Self is not able to really "think" outside—or experience anything outside—of what is taking place within all of these reactive mechanisms and so forth. Because what the Reactive Control Center does is really send up "mental images"—these imprinted images. We talk about *imprints* a lot; I mean, everyone kind of knows what an imprint is: it's this "stamped image" so to speak.

When you "imprint" something, you're strongly impressing or marking it onto something that's considered impressionable—some softer surface. And you're marking it with pressure onto a surface. And so, for example, in our Systemology, we use this to describe the *imprinting* as the type of, for example, "mental imagery" and its "emotional encoding" that keeps one in that "figure-8" cycle of reactivity, with anything that's regarding emotional distress or pain or unconsciousness—anything that's antagonistic to, you know, the "survival" of the individual, particularly as a "physical being" when we're talking about the reactivity of the genetic vehicle.

We know that the Alpha-Spirit is able to *supersede this existence* and obviously lives more than one lifetime—but when we're talking about survival and we're talking about survival in *this* lifetime, we're talking about the "Game" we're playing right now; we're talking about any kind of threat that might trigger the reactive-response mechanisms that we've formerly only considered, you know, like the "fight or flight responses." This is what imprinting is.

Imprinting—when we're talking about knowledge and associative data and so forth, we're talking about the Mind, we're talking about programming programming and *thought*. When we're talking about things connected to pain and loss and emotional experiences of distress and trauma, we're talking about *emotion*—you know, the response mechanisms that are triggered at an emotional level, specifically concerning the environment of the physical genetic organism.

As a higher level of Awareness and as operating, being an Alpha-Spirit, knowing that we are dealing with energies and not necessarily what the physical objects around us are —we're dealing with the *impressions* of energy and matter that's, you know, vastly condensed at this physical beta-existence—but we know that energy vibrations and even thoughts *can* have the ability to not only affect our own reactive-control mechanisms and imprinting and restimulation of various things, but also *others*.

We were talking *in the previous lecture* about the old idea of "group consciousness" and stuff, so—particularly if they are sharing that level of reality or agreements to the same degree. Even when they're not. There's many points of experience when we, you know, can spot where these *other* realities or other *personal universes* and the solidity of them has been impressed upon us or enforced upon us.

And this is something you see even in "social programming" and so forth—and it's just part of the basic civic circuits of systematization that has been going on as part of civilization since the inception of all this thousands of years ago in Babylon. And that's one of the reasons why we study *those* systems then, too.

All throughout the Mardukite Master Course—whether we're talking about the structure of the Elemental Tech, or we're talking about the manner of which societies were programmed by priest-classes and Dragon-Kings and so forth—we're talking about "*systems*" every step of the way. We are examining within this—which is why we call it the Mardukite Academy of Systemology—we are looking at the "*systems*" of things, and as a result of this type of systematic logic, we are actually able to glean a much higher understanding and a clearer understanding that is able to be shared and communicated; and that an individual doesn't need to spend decades of their life held up in some university library in order to understand.

So, I mean, really—it's not our goal to change the fact that basic systems exists; nor is it to throw up our hands in defeat and go: "Well, I guess that's that." These systems are all *dynamic*. And they are subject to our participation—though that participation is always going to be defined by our level of understanding and Awareness and our willingness to reach and actually apply the creative abilities of Self to this participation and experience of life.

This becomes—when we're talking about the idea that an individual in beta-existence is basically... the functional purpose is to continue that exist. When we talk about the functional purpose or Utilitarian purpose at a spiritual level, really the highest function or purpose of an Alpha-Spirit would be: *to create.*

It's really up to the individual to be in charge of the creation of their own personal Universe *and* their participation in the Universe of the "Game" at large.

Clearly, it's also been observed how, like, solidified thoughts —those that are given a lot of energy and mass and so forth —that are intensely broadcast have the ability or tendency even to be carried and built upon by others that are affected by them or that interact with them.

Even when an individual is *opposed* to an idea—even when someone is like, doesn't really want to be in agreement on the position of it—there's still something now in existence for us to have a position to be in agreement with *at all*.

And so, the Standard Model really demonstrates that our thoughts are creating vibrations and various frequencies, and this is what's demonstrated on the ZU-line—what constitutes the variations of our structure of what the ZU-line is doing. It is *Self* engaging with the world around us, which is basically waveforms relative to our own vibrations—and this produces a particular result or state or consequence and has a particular "energetic signature" or "wave frequency pattern" and that is what is being interpreted—and *that* is what is given significance or other associative data and so forth.

That's what's taking place out there in the world around— or in the existence or "world" or "Universe" or what have you—is it's a series of *waves*; each one of these carrying a specific signature at various conditions that has a specific... Once you have a certain experience or whatnot, you begin to give it certain classifications and so they're later identified based on that.

So, the individual is basically trained in Systemology how to properly manage and handle the "Mind-System"—that's one of the functional purposes of it; doing so, not from the idea that you're a "human animal with this weird brain going on, with all these kind of things happening to it and so forth and you can't really have much responsibility for."

We're looking at it from the fact that there is an "*Alpha-Spirit*" outside—or exterior to—this beta-existence, that has the ability to basically operate, much like you would with a joystick for a game or a keyboard or something, to operate this human experience.

And so, really, when we deal with "*processing*," we're dealing with an individual consciously and willingly, from the Alpha-Spirit perspective, basically working through their command of the "Mind-System." And this is quite different from unknowingly going through life and operating on the predisposed cycles and patterns, where they're just continuously reinforced, you know, the thoughtforms, the imprints, the fragments of reality—the solidity is reinforced when they're given this *new attention* or given an emotional charge *by* the reactive-responses.

Now, if an individual goes back to a point, for example—if you go *back* to a point that was unpleasant and you consciously sit and decide to go back and work it through and analyze it and work it through several times, looking at various facets of it and you're willingly consciously doing that from, you know, a *grounded* "tranquil" state of mind, than you're actually able to undo a lot of the negative affects of that.

However, when you are operating simply at lower-levels of Awareness out in mundane beta-existence—average everyday reality of the world—and various facets—what we refer to as facets, different aspects that are contained within those memories—get restimulated by the environment outside of your control, outside the control of the individual, *that* fragmentation, *that* imprinting, gets solidified.

And not only does it trigger various response-mechanisms and mess with that "present point" of *Awareness*, when the experience is being had and managed, but it actually solidifies and makes stronger this reactivity—these patterns and cycles—where rather than being in charge of one's experience, rather than being in control of the Mind and being able to manage the "mental images" and what kind of emotions that we are choosing to feel—because, we can actually *choose* to feel those; those aren't just all push-button mechanisms there if one is Self-Honest and reached defragmentation.

But, we're working to establish a point where there is no longer these reactive mechanisms; and as long as we're allowing—one way or another an individual is going to experience and they are being programmed or conditioned or having "Mind-Systems" generate various dynamics that are carried with us. Obviously they affect—we've agreed somehow that they affect us and we carry that with us.

But, obviously this encoding—I mean, it can stay dormant for a long time without resurfacing; but, when it's restimulated in the environment outside of Self-determinism, this consistently brings one's *beta-Awareness*—the state of *Awareness* operating in *this* existence—lower and lower along the course of their lifetime. And it's really been my observation that this is one of the things that contributes to the degradation of the considerations of Self as the *body* ages.

Because, again, the failure to understand *time*, failure to understand *cycles* and failure to understand the *abilities* and the *purpose* of *Self* and essentially its journey and its adventure as it has basically been doing what it's been doing for however long, you know, it's been in existence. We're talking about *defragmentation* here; and this is "clearing the slate"—getting an individual back to a point of functionality as Self; and then whatever they choose to do with their life, well at least they're freely choosing to do so.

The painful memories—whether it's physical, emotional, mental; however... it only has to be *perceived*, these threats, the type of imprinting that can trigger them or cause them, it just has to be a *perceived* threat to survival or endangerment. It doesn't have to be a full unconsciousness or trauma

—it could even be the threat *of* or restimulation of a point *of.*

But, this—what this does, when this... what others would refer to as "conditioning" —this ends up, essentially, treating it.. or, *keeping* an individual, their point of Awareness, kind of stuck or suspended in these lower-levels of Awareness; and this is how they're essentially operating their experience of the Human Condition afterward. You know, we treat this—anything for long periods, you know, severely —under the point of "2" on the Standard Model; and then (we treat) how that evolves into the *beta-Awareness* when we treat "*Crystal Clear.*"

We basically say that this type of information—the type of information that is stored as an *imprint* is the "emotional encoding" of these experiences. Much as you would put something "analytical" or a fixed piece of "data" into memory as a thought, we're talking about, basically, something that is almost—it's *lower* than thought, because it's a restimulation of an almost artificial environment that's meant to substitute the scenery of what is taking place in the physical environment, in beta-existence at that given time.

So, we refer to it as an "imprint"—so, if you were to imagine, like, a "glass slate" and you're making a holographic image upon it whenever something is imprinted on it—such as a period of pain, or a loss, or something that takes place where an individual feels a danger or threat to their survival as a physical organism—this is imprinted on this slate and stored, essentially, in the "*Reactive Control Center,*" which is accessed *prior to* the analytical thoughts and the mode of thinking controlled by the upper-levels of the Mind-System whenever the association is encountered.

Rather than, you know, you see something—and you see a "car," and so your thought is going: "Oh, well, that's a car; and a car is a vehicle and has four wheels"; or it could be a different level of Awareness, like: "That's a shiny red car" or "That's a Buick." Whatever it is—each level of Awareness would have obviously had different associations with that; whether a person is interested or enthusiastic or whatever, those are all states of Mind—and we can actually gauge all those, systematically, using the *Beta-Awareness Scale* in *"Crystal Clear."*

But, when we're dealing with the emotional reactive levels —the (emotionally encoded) imprints—than these slates of information are actually not so much about "analytical information" in respect of *thought*, but rather (emotional) *imprints* that include *facets* that are not just scenery, but it could be anything—it could be the smells that are in the air at the time; it could be of quality of light in the environment; or the type of dust or humidity in the room—you know, the quality in the room; the position of the body, even.

All of these different things get basically "etched" into this "imprint" and are stored as a memory that way—and with *emotional* attachment to it; so that when this type of stuff is pulled into, you know, the "Mind-System" later, as a treatment of reality, it's these *imprints* that are being treated rather than "analytical thought." And the more validation— or the deeper the imprinting—is over time received, without being defragmented: well, those imprints are, of course, just getting stronger and stronger.

And so, these *facets*, like I said, have a tendency to *defy* "analytical" or "logical" thinking. In this respect, an individual might see the "car" and suddenly be shown the experience —or almost *relive* the experience, even if not visually in the mind, than emotionally—some kind of traumatic experience regarding "cars."

So, I mean this is—it could be as simple as this. And this could eventually get to a point where, honestly, even going outside and seeing "cars" could give them the feeling where they're "sick"; and then they don't want to go outside anymore, they don't want to deal with people or cars—and they start to withdraw from society and so and so forth and just kind of, you know...

You can easily see the downward spiral that just kind of accumulates when these patterns and cycles just continue to be validated as they are without any point of *defragmentation.*

Now, what we've learned to do in Systemology—and what is kind of demonstrated and referred to in Mardukite Systemology "*Liber-One,*" which is "The Tablets of Destiny" and it's also contained in your "*Systemology Handbook*" Grade-III textbook for this course—is the idea that: in a proper state of Awareness, good state of Mind, when we are not experiencing emotional reactivity, or with the assistance, for example, of a "Pilot" or someone else even—just even a friend or that's knowledgeable; it's helpful if they are at least *aware* of this kind of material, too, even if it isn't trained expert piloting—with the idea that combined *Awareness* and attention on whatever kind of imprinting that has taken place, it can basically be resurfaced intentionally and brought through, you know, an individual can go through it and do like what we were saying: bringing certain thoughts to mind, or certain experiences or imprints to mind, intentionally while one's grounded, and then actually go through them and work through them.

And an individual can be assisted in that simply by having *extra* Awareness applied to the situation; by having someone that's there to basically assist and help them in that. And this isn't something that requires a whole lot of, you know, expertise, energy and attention to do at a primitive level—and that's why it's relayed in "*The Tablets of Destiny,*" which isn't even a "*pilot handbook,*" such as we see, for example, with "*Metahuman Destinations,*" which is geared more toward "Piloted Procedure."

But, yeah, I mean at the very least actualization—total Master Control—at least of the "Mind-System"—beta-defragmentation—what we treat up to, you know, "4.0" on the Standard Model or the *Beta Awareness Scale*, the Master Control Center. I mean this is kind of a critical component to *any* further, you know, "levels of Awareness" or ability to *Actualize* or progress any further on a *Pathway to Self-Honesty* or the *Gateways to Infinity*.

Because, beyond Grade-III, we're referring to "Wizard Levels," we're referring to "Wizard Grades"—we're referring to someone that has already achieved a masterful understanding and handling of all that we've been treating in this course and these materials leading up to that—and this is what is defining what we're treating as... I mean, forget "transhumanism," *this* is what we're treating as *metahumanism*: the total control of the Mind-System, handling the Mind-System and the functional command of the Human Condition or *any* genetic vehicle for beta-existence.

This is the key component to what we have seen as a reflection of "gods" or "Ascended Masters" or, you know, anything that we've seen of this nature all throughout history; we look all throughout what we've covered in the Mardukite Master Course and Grade-I and Grade-II: *6,000 years of recorded history*, where we have seen elements of just a select few individuals that *have* stood apart from the rest and somehow the efforts of that—or the keys or techniques behind that—seemed to have been lost along the way, or not perfectly duplicated in order to deliver these same states to others. This duplication factor not being met in the past is one of the purposes of the Mardukite Master Course.

If we're talking about the high degrees of *Actualization*, beta-experience and the Human Condition and being able to treat the experience of control of thought and really experiencing life for all the vibrancy that it can—far and above the norm—this is where we are reaching that; we are reaching that with Grade-III.

And although, yeah, we've alluded to these concepts, and we've been striving and reaching toward this all along the steps of the way, through the first three tiers of our *ascent* up the "Ladder of Lights" or the "pyramid" or the "ziggurat"—the *Stairway to Heaven* or the *Gateways to Infinity*—this is the point when we're actually *seeing* those results.

And that's what defines the break-point between a "Master-Level" understanding and a higher "Wizard-Level" or *actualized* expertise *in* these applications.

In one of the lectures *yesterday*, I just kind of briefly brushed across the Three Principle Systems of Cosmic Manifestation, which is what's described on the "Arcane Tablets." They're referred to as: *substance*, *motion* and *consciousness*. And, of course, these conditions of Awareness, you can understanding them—we're making the comparisons to "physical systems," "mental systems" and "spiritual systems."

But, again, when we refer to that, we're referring to almost like the gradients along the scale, for example, the ZU-line or the Standard Model—because these principles, they're just representative of certain qualities of the states of systems, you know, we refer to them as ranges, for example, of like the "physical" or whatnot.

For example, you could consider "Physical Substance" as "Matter" and then also there could be "Emotional Substance"—like, the idea that "substance" is only "matter" is not what we mean. Because you could have, for example, "Emotional Substance" being an "Imprint"—or a "Mental Substance" being a "Thoughtform." So, I mean, every "state" is a "condition" of manifestation within each of the energetic ranges.

That's why even though we have a systematic understanding of the relationships of things, it's important that we don't substitute one thing for another—or one concept for another—just because they *might* correlate a little bit.

For example, we might say something like "substance"—but, you know, all the Principle Systems of Cosmic Manifestation are expressions of, one way or another, like what we were talking about before, just *energy*. And whether you're talking about the *flow* or the communication of information, we're talking about *energy*, just at its most basic state.

Just as people, you know—you're most likely to relate the concept of "substance" to the "physical." For example, *bodies* or *matter* as an application of energy. The Principle Systems of Motion—you know, when you think of activity, yeah, we can directly equate that to the Mind; because when you think of *energy in action* and mental thought and so forth.

But, wherever a condition of *substance* exists, there's also going to be a condition of *motion* and then, you know, *consciousness* to observe it and so forth. These are kind of broad terms, you know: *energy, frequency, vibration*—we're referring to "motion" and "action" and basically *affinity* in regard to all things...

What is "affinity"? Well, we do define that, first and foremost, in *"The Tablets of Destiny."* There's also the "Systemology NexGen Glossary" in the *"Instructor's Manual"* and in the appendix of *"Systemology Handbook."* So, any of the terms, as we are using them, or any terms that have a specific application *in* Systemology are actually found in that glossary.

But—"Affinity" *is* the "apparent and energetic relationship between substances or bodies" or the "degree of attraction or repulsion between things based on natural forces" or the "similitude or differences of waveforms or the connection between systems."

In terms of the average individual, or the Human Condition, "affinity" can sometimes just be considered similar to "liking"; things that we "like" have a tendency to be something we are attracted toward or we would wish to have close to us and so forth. So, when we talk about something having "affinity" with something, it has a particular connection—particularly even systematically.

When you look at the "Arcane Tablet" lore—you look at any of the sciences even today—it's gonna show that, you know, the "Cosmos"—Cosmic Power, for example—whatever we're witnessing, for example, in the *Enuma Eliš*—the Tablets of Creation—we're seeing a "*motion*" of things; like all things in the Cosmos operating as a state of motion; and this idea of rate and frequency—the degree of motion—this is what, you know, when people talk about "vibrations" or "energy" or even the state of where something is at on the ZU-line and Standard Model, this is what we're talking about.

This goes back to an ancient—the Ancient Mystery School—or Hermetic Axiom that: "Nothing rests. Everything moves; everything vibrates." And we find *energy* in *action* all throughout the Standard Model, all throughout the ZU-line, all throughout our consideration of anything in existence—everything between *zero* and *Infinity*.

And of course, we've brought up in the Master Course, about "polarity" and "duality" being the basis of "motion"—*that* differential being what causes energy to flow. And so we have "physical material" and "physical systems," that's gonna gravitate toward the point of slowest possible "vibration" or "frequency" at the physical state.

And this is basically the "entropy" of the continuity of the physical beta-existence that we treat at *Zero*, or that's given the cuneiform sign KI—to indicate the Earth or the Physical; that direction on the Standard model.

And then "Spiritual Matter" and "spiritual material" in "Spiritual Systems" gravitates towards the point of the highest possible spiritual vibration—and this in the direction of *Infinity*, or the direction of AN—the "star-sign" that we use for Mardukite Zuism, or the "cross." And to this dynamic, I've used the word "extropy," which is not actually a word, but it *should be*. [*Laughs.*]

The "pull" from both of these aspects of the "dichotomy" *is* the force that excites, essentially, the *motion* and *activity* of what's treated as the condition of substance; and so you see the substance, the action and then, of course, the consciousness that is there to observe it and give it significance.

And "consciousness"—I mean, we don't dismiss that, because it's the third Principle System of Manifestation. It's literally the activity of the Self, the Observer, the I-AM—that which is doing the observing. And you know, Descartes referred to "I think, therefore I am"—*but*, that's not even fully accurate. It's the I-AM, the actual Self—Alpha-Spirit—is able to *observe the thinking.* It is the one that can observe the thinking.

It is not the one *doing* the thinking or *having* the thinking—it can actually *control* and observe the thinking from outside of it. Of course, if your considerations are fixed to [*laughs*] beta-condition or beta-existence *as* the Human Condition, than of course, than yeah, I guess, than you're "up in your mind."

And some people aren't *even* up in their Mind—they're stuck in the *body* somewhere, you know. They're still having the experience—still attached to the experience—or having the experience generated around them of the point of loss or the point of pain or whatever imprinting has taken place. And so those people are often just essentially stuck in their bodies.

Actually, *not even* that much—essentially wanting nothing to do *with*, no responsibility, nothing to do with their body, because of the pain and withdrawal from that.

And then you have other people that are, essentially, stuck

in their "head," because of "mental programming" and "implants" and certain thought *considerations* that are basically keeping them within certain circular *loops* at *that* level.

Of course, the goal being to get someone actualized as a *Spirit*—into Self as a Spirit—but, some people haven't even gotten (up) into their (own) head enough to process them to get out of their heads.

So, at the lowest level of work in Systemology—before we're talking about "processing" individuals to be able to handle these various things and those various things and all these different patterns and flows and the total management of *Life* and so forth, we're talking about a *basic* gradient here of getting someone *back* in control and communication with the "*body*," in command and control of the "*Mind*" and actualized as the "*Spirit*." And an individual that isn't even "in" their Mind *yet*, what exactly—what is it that you are even processing?

So to recap here: we've got the Systems of Manifestations—these Principle Systems—that kind of philosophically correspond to basic Conditions of Awareness as they are aligned on the Standard Model—Physical, Mental and Spiritual. And then the examination of each of these systems reveals that the same three Principles of apparent manifestation are actually in operation at each level. So, you have *consciousness, action* and *substance* appearing at spiritual levels, mental levels, physical levels and so forth. And we call "physical" or "physical matter" is only the lowest manifested vibrations of Cosmic Energy that are interacting with "consciousness."

And then the Principle of "substance" is what distinguishes things as "bodies"—what gives "things" *form* as "things." That's why "things" *are* "things." That's what the Substance Principle is—not strictly just "bodies" as *bodies* or masses in that respect. Whenever a condition of substance exists, we have a condition of motion to be found; because, we are talking about the flow of energy. We are talking about matter—even concrete matter—has a flow of energy. All things in the Cosmos have some state of motion.

When we broadly apply terms like *energy* and *frequency* and stuff, we're talking about, essentially, the *action*; we're talking about—in regards to Cosmic Motion—we're also talking about the "affinity" of things; we're talking about "things" in *relationship* to other "things." The third Principle being, of course, "consciousness" or *Awareness*—it's the activity of Self; and the point of the Observer—the "I"—you can't eliminate [*laughs*] that from the equation.

All communications and expressions of *consciousness* as reality in manifestation are an *activity* between two or more forms or bodies. This dichotomy is what allows for the flow —and then in terms of *consciousness*, we have to have something in relation to something else. And even this relationship, because of the distance between them, gives us in some respects, the concept of "*Time*" because there is "*Space*"—and "space" and "distance" gives us the concept of "time." So, we don't eliminate that from the equation either.

The idea of "affinity" would be basically what we are willing or interested or would find enjoyable to have with us in "present time" or in a close vicinity in space. And so, what we don't have an affinity with is that which is, you know, we wish to keep away from us and have no communications with.

There you see—I mean, that's about the extent, when you look at the Hermetic Principles, that's about as far as a lot of individuals have ever been able to determine, concerning Hermetic Philosophy and what's been drawn forth from the Arcane Tablets. And you can see evidence of this information, actually, on the "Tablet-O" and "Tablet-T" series in Grade-II and the "*Anunnaki Bible.*"

: LECTURE 44—BETA-DEFRAGMENTATION :
(September 29, 2020)

[*We've been talking about the fundamentals of Mardukite Systemology—what we classify as Grade-III, concerning the Master-Levels of the work—the work of Mardukite Systemology; the work of the Mardukite Master Course. And this is—I'm kind of excited to be able to deliver this at all. We've never really given any presentations of the general concept of Systemology other than the work that I was doing—the workshops—for each of the individual book releases: "The Tablets of Destiny" and "Crystal Clear." And that was nearly a year ago. And everything that I've been pretty much focused on for 2020 has pretty much been geared toward "Grade-IV" and "Piloting" and so forth. And this—these fundamentals of Systemology, I mentioned in a previous lecture that we might make some of this material required, some of these lectures, required listening when it comes to even Mardukite Ministers; not just "Pilots" of Systemology, but even the Mardukite Ministers—the Ministers within Mardukite Zuism, as we develop that further.*]

Because really, for the times being what they are, it is just as important to understand and be able to apply our Mardukite Systemology as it is to understand the basis and structure and semantics from, like, ancient Mesopotamia—and for example, the whole track of what has led to this point, which we have explored in, for example, in Grade-I and Grade-II. And we've been exploring these fundamentals, essentially, as they've been set forth or developed over the last decade—everything—we've been going back to "*The Original Thesis*" work nearly a decade ago, and what's led up to this point.

The emphasis at this juncture—and what we'll close off this lecture for the rest of the day—we're looking at the materials from "*The Systemology Handbook*" and materials that compose that; we're getting a concise illumination highlighting the specific points that are necessary to draw from, for example, the material in Mardukite *Liber-One*, "*The Tablets of Destiny*"—and of course, that material is also in your "*Systemology Handbook.*"

We have had success with individuals working with "*Crystal Clear*" directly—even prior to examining "*The Tablets of Destiny.*" It really just depends (on) how motivated and actualized an individual already is. Of course, we've found that it is far easier to take an individual that's already pretty much "able"—an individual that's already worked through the previous, kind of rigamarole of life, and is already a point where they already kind of know and are ready to accept a lot of these higher principles; as opposed to, basically, trying to take an individual and introduce them with all of the "metaphysics" and "higher spiritual tech" and concepts that are attached to Systemology.

Of course, we are actively, actually, working more and more every day on developing such a delivery—not only using "Mardukite Zuism" as an entry point to our Systemology, but also ways in which can actually work and define many elements of Systemology...

Of course, I'm now currently involved with getting "upper Grades" established, but for example, we have individuals on our Publication Staff and other members who—*some even here today*—that are working on synthesizing, for example, taking excerpts out of the lectures, and taking various aspects from the book releases, and synthesizing introductory material and so forth.*

Because as far as I'm concerned—the "Wizard Levels" and "Wizard Grades" and upper-level work of Systemology and

---

* The first of these introductory compilations appeared in early 2021, shortly after the Mardukite Master Course was delivered—"*The Way Into The Future: A Handbook for Humanity*"—based on the work by Joshua Free, as edited by James Thomas.

so forth—as far as I'm concerned: all of that is just as *pie in the sky* for an individual as anything else *until* you've actually come up to a point where you can reach it; where it's actually something you have a reality on.

That is actually, you know—all of what we're trying to fine tune in "Wizard Levels," we are actually reaching certain points of that already in Grade-III; and so, an individual already should be able to—almost intuitively—figure on what the next aspect of the *Pathway* is on their own, had they actually completed and worked through the "systematic processing" and instruction that's intended for a Grade-III understanding of Mardukite Systemology.

One of the reasons that the "upper Grades"—the work for them—is now moving so expeditiously, is because we've been able to take all of what *works*, for example, what has been relayed in the Mardukite Master Course and the highlights of that—the pitfalls; the truths—and we've been able to take all of what works and now move forward, almost independent of the type of stuff that's been done before and mainstream "New Age" work and so forth.

And this is actually as a result of such a strong foundation, such as these tiers established in the Mardukite Master Course—these first three Grades. It's the—the way ahead moves a lot quicker for us now at the Mardukite Academy and the Systemology Society, because we're *working at it*; we're working at it every day—the practical aspects of it—finding effective methodology behind this "spiritual philosophy" and what we're considering "spiritual tech"—"technology" or "techniques."

This is far different than the type of work we have done in the past, which was primarily the result of a lot of intensive "New Age" *initiation-work* and various research and looking to see what all these other groups were doing and the legacy that has extended through Europe, and digging up all these tablets in Mesopotamia and so forth—*yeah*, we've established that. We've got these textbooks now that establish *that* material.

But the way ahead is not really built upon the—the pathway ahead is not built upon the rocks and rubble of yesterday's ruin. We are—we're forging and creating a *new* pathway that has *never* before been explored or demonstrated effectively in the past 6,000 years.

Yeah, you know, Systemology and the semantics and the vocabulary behind it—and attaching it to Mardukite Zuism—and all of this stuff seems incredibly *new*; and that's okay—that's what the Mardukite Master is there to help, kind of, usher in. Because, if we had just basically redid or repackaged what had already been done before, this would be—that would be entirely pointless.

We could have very easily done that; we could have very easily stuck with Grade-I type work or we could have fixed all of our attentions on what was Grade-II and treated that as the *end*, but I'm *still* here, you're *still* here, we're still working at all this—we're showing that there is a progressive pathway that meets specific goals and specific ideals each step of the way and we're continuing to move forward.

So, when we consider the work that's presented in "*The Tablets of Destiny*," we are looking at, essentially, the inception of the "Mardukite Systemology"—*modern* Mardukite Systemology—as it's being presented to the public today. I know that we've had Alumni and Mardukite Chamberlains and various individuals involved in the Systemological Society as it existed in the *underground* for nearly a decade.

But where it comes to our presentation today—where it comes to the way that we're treating the history of the development and so forth today—this inception essentially begins; well, we released "*The Tablets of Destiny*" for Halloween or Samhain in 2019. And prior to that, there really was very little information—very little attention given—on a surface level, concerning for example, our publications, our blogging, the videos and so forth—very little attention had been given to Systemology on a public level.

In the process of developing what we were planning, that was basically when we made a resurgence—the tenth anniversary of the "Mardukites," the establishment of our own independent publishing company, which supersedes the distribution and we are producing hardcovers now that are publicly available, not just the prearranged numbered limited editions that were actually quite expensive back in the day; we're now able to distribute hardcovers and materials all over the globe and through a multiplicity of distributors. We're able to reach more individuals that way and get more people involved on the web.

I'm going to be focusing more on independent websites and independent web work rather than social networking over the next decade—so that we can establish a little bit more of our own presence and our own brand and not be relying on these other channels to do so. So, yeah...

"*The Tablets of Destiny*"—it's establishing a bridge between Grade-II and Grade-III and this is why we were able to move into it using the *Enuma Eliš* and other examples from the Arcane Tablets and ancient cuneiform sources as our pivot point—as our point of entry into this.

The other purpose "*The Tablets of Destiny*" is to refine the introductory relay of our understanding—our understanding of Self and our understanding of the Universes and basically the environment around us; the "set" that *we* are occupying, or demonstrating and the "setting" in which it's being applied to and that interactive point. This is the—that kind of relationship is what we consider, you know, the "systematic" nature of reality and so forth. It's those two points coming together.

And then we were finally able to establish this with our Standard Model, which—the Standard Model now, I mean, it's been a concept... I mean, we're calling it the Standard Model and the ZU-line and all of that—these concepts have been tried... Attempts have been made to present this level of understanding for *thousands* of years.

You can find remnants and elements of our Standard Model in the, for example, well, we've talked about the "StarGates"—the "Gate" system of ancient Mesopotamia—and of course, its later development as the Semitic Kabbalah; we've established that there's a relationship in terms of the connection between these layers and what the individual has assumed or taken on as considerations for the Human experience or the Human Condition; we've made connections to the chakras with that information.

In terms of the cosmology of these "Spheres": the concepts behind them run very similarly to the "Druid's Cabala" and the establishment of the philosophy that was relayed by them concerning the various "Spheres of Existence." I mean, you could go on and on and on finding all of the parallels—and that's essentially what makes this Standard Model for our Systemology *actually functional.*

It demonstrates with a simplicity of understanding and a minimal amount of mathematics and physics and so forth—concepts to understand in order to relay, for example, that all physical and spiritual manifestation is encompassed with this cosmology, basically composed of the ALL and the LAW; and it demonstrates that continuum of Infinity Energy, which we call ZU, which connects the Spiritual Systems to the Physical Systems, essentially, as *Life.*

And it demonstrates that *beyond Life* and *outside the LAW* and *encompassing the ALL* is but Infinity—and that is relayed very simplistically on the Standard Model.

Now, the divisions of the Standard Model and the way in

which the ZU-line is impressed upon it and so forth—now, this is all based on basic logics and the symbols attributed to it are just, kind of, for simplicity. Otherwise, this is a very simple model to relay; and it's not very esoteric. It shows an Infinity, which consists of Nothingness, outside of near-infinite potentiality, which is the ALL, for example, starting at "7": consisting of the Spiritual Universe, the actual spiritual potential of ALL existence—and that composes what we also refer to as the direction of AN—a spiritual existence or Alpha-existence relative to what is separated by the LAW, which defines physical existence or beta-existence of the Physical Universe—which is what we consider any manifest... the potential of the Physical Universe as you are experiencing it, all the way down to its inert continuity as matter.

And this seems kind of—this may seem like: "Oh, well, so what?" But, if you examine, for example, the information in *"The Tablets of Destiny"* and especially as we apply it to our parameters of what we consider "beta-defragmentation"— we are using this model to understand our Self, the world around us, all of the considerations that have been made by Self, all of the considerations that have been made to define and restrict and condense physical existence—this beta-existence—that we are occupying; and then as tool—as a *Key*— just as the "Ladder of Lights" in ancient Mesopotamia, or the way in which some individuals have attempted to use different versions of the Kabbalah: *this is*, essentially, the "Road-Map Out."

In regards to the ZU-line—or in regards to the emanation of Self, or the point of Beingness that Self is using as point-of-view or a consideration for and as Self; because, again, most people, we were talking in the *previous* lecture about some individuals almost wanting to have nothing to do with the *body*, then alone being stuck in a *body* or stuck in a *head* and so forth—what we're talking about here; from the *other way* —we're talking about an Alpha Awareness, the Alpha-Spirit as basically an Awareness point.

So, we're treating Self as essentially an Awareness, okay? And so, Alpha Awareness is extending as ZU—as an energy—from the direction of AN or Infinity, in Alpha Existence along the ZU-line and *contacting* beta-existence in the direction of KI, or the Physical Existence. And this is essentially experienced as the manifestation of the genetic body—the experience *of* being, you know, essentially attached *to* the Human Condition in this lifetime.

I mean, when we were identifying the most ancient concepts of, for example, Mardukite Zuism and the whole purpose for the name for it, we found that they had actually identified this "spirit" or "Self-Awareness" or the "spiritual consciousness of Self" as "ZU." And so, that seemed to work perfectly fine for our purposes. We've covered its relationship—the concept of Zuism—in relation to other traditions and other applications of it, but that's the whole purpose behind *our* application of the term "ZU."

And this *"lifeforce"*—or "spiritual energy"—it's a *constant* wherever it is; and that's probably why it's rarely detectable within the range of the Physical Universe. The universe is relying on "motion" or some kind of "activity" in order for the calculations to take place.

Some individuals have this idea that, for example, that ZU somehow would "diminish" in "lifeforce"—or that the "lifeforce" or "spirit" or concept of Self somehow "diminishes" as more time goes on, or as "life" progresses in this existence—but that's not really the case. And what we've been describing is that it actually gets entangled or wrapped up into these *imprints* or various *emotional masses* and so forth along the *line*, which is carried as what the individual is considering as themselves.

[*A gap in the original masters occurs here to remove a period of silence and background noise during a statement made by a student, inaudible to the recordings.*]

Yeah, that's probably why they haven't understood much about ZU or *Self* or *consciousness*—and why, even our ZU-line, if you don't place it as an interaction with the Standard Model of Universes and their correlated energy and matter —it's basically in a state of constant potential.

So, when the currents—when the energy—hits against something, we have manifestation; something to be aware of. So, now, we have this various manifestation happening with ourselves to various degrees; and manifestation taking place wherever our *Awareness* comes into contact with some type of sensory stimulation or anything that's, you know, in our environment. That's really the only way we know that something *is*. A part of us, or waves, or fields—it's bumping up against a part of *it*. And whatever we determine of this, that's kind of our *reality*.

And so, the ZU is coming in, essentially, into the system as a *constant* from *Self*—*Self* being a Source here. It's probably not the "Absolute Source," which is why we look to the direction of Infinity—but, it's a *constant*. And whenever it's not being, you know, delivered in "full force" to that part of the spectrum that's reaching the physical *body*, then there is some kind of *solid* diverting that path of energy, absorbing it, making it more solid.

This is why everything is experienced the way it is; particularly things that are "thought" or "conceived" in the Mind, or stimulating "mental images"—or any kind of "emotional reactivity" and "emotional responses." An individual— you're rarely having a clear interaction with the environment *as* its energetic nature, as the *flow* and *ebb* and *tides* of all these *streams* and *currents*. It's being received and interpreted through all these *channels* and *networks* and "sensory wiring" in order to project what is taking place—what the individual *is* experiencing around them as *reality*. And *that* is a projection that comes from *Self*.

You may not be making all the energies out there taking place, *but* when you put *your* Awareness out on them and interact with them and "encounter" them, *you* are the one that's actually setting up the "mental image"—the experience that you're having—what you're seeing; what you're sensing. That's self-generated. And that is where the energy that comes in—that's basically unlimited, coming in at full potential—it comes in and basically gets wrapped up *in* to the types of solids and masses and imprinting and programming that an individual, basically, is carrying with them as "devices"—as "mechanisms"—to generate the *reality* that they're experiencing.

When we talk about "*beta-defragmentation*," we're talking about defragmenting the diversion—the diverted path—of this energy, in terms of these "mechanisms" that are concerned *with* the experience of beta-existence—those connected specifically to the genetic vehicle, the emotional channels, all of the associated thought that's gone into the way an individual categorizes and sorts their experience— all of this is basically treated as "*defragmentation*." The opposite of it, being "*fragmented.*"

We're basically, you know, *clearing* the *crystal*—or "healing the crystal" so to speak; to use some archaic fantasy language. What we ended up resulting in—as far as this work— very quickly after putting it together for "*The Tablets of Destiny*" was "*Crystal Clear*," which is a "self-processing" manual that also appears within "*The Systemology Handbook.*"

So, these imprints—or these emotional masses—that we treat when we're talking about the "Reactive Control Center," when we're talking about emotional imprinting—and these emotional "solids" that seem to *hold* or *contain* the energy that seems to bring an individual "down" as they travel farther on their journey. These would almost be equivalent to—if we're treating an equivalency to the range of thought —these would be similar to "*beliefs.*"

But they don't necessarily have a *rational* component; they're simply the entire picture or "snapshot" of the emotional experience as it was received—or perceived—in every aspect. So, anything caught in the range of view of perception becomes a *facet* or a *component* of the "imprint." And this can include completely arbitrary and irrational associations.

I mean, this is—the idea of "associative knowledge" and its effect—this has been treated only loosely in the past, concerning for example, the idea of "conditioning." But, we know that "conditioning"—it's really these "*imprints*" that are being treated here; because they have a component to them that is far more than just a basic "reactive-response mechanism."

These imprints contain facets that aren't even logically associated with the incident—and these can be "restimulated." We've discovered that the entire concept really—well, there's an "energetic" aspect to what is considered "conditioning" and this can be described within our Systemology, concerning "ZU" and the premise of the "imprint."

This is just for *our* Systemology—I mean, the idea of "imprinting" and so forth has had *other* associations in other schools of thought. So, we're particularly concerned with *our* application *in* Systemology of, basically, how emotional information is stored and how it can have the ability to override more logical analytical information that is treated at higher levels on the "ZU-line."

I mean, it's not all "mysterious." Certainly, there are certain layers that an individual is *not* aware of; and these are probably some of the greater sources of personal fragmentation. But, you know, if you examine these various facets of an experience —and we treat this more intensely in the "*Crystal Clear*" volume—but if you examine these in your past, in your own past experience, there's many times when I'm sure you've been *aware* that something happening or something in your environment reminds you of something else and are identified with it.

And this kind of *identification*, of course, is considered erroneous when it comes to higher levels of thought; because, we can misappropriate the idea of fear or danger or loss—we can apply all of these past experiences to our present circumstances even when there's no logical reason to do so; and this begins to affect the clarity of thought, and in turn, all the way down to the actual actions—the behaviors—of an individual, and affect what they are actually willing to do.

Unfortunately, in the case of "emotional imprinting," the idea is that anything kinda caught in the frame of perception could be associated with the same originally encoded threat or event, and then later, any of these facets, if they catch the light of our Awareness in the future—or presented in the environment—they get, what we consider, "restimulated."

And you can even see this for example, when we talked about the "Figure-8" loop, and just the idea that an individual is kinda "sling-shotting" between a particular mental state and an emotional state, very often this is because of an association—those two states have been associated together. A certain facet of the environment, or a certain mode of thought, or a certain idea—or something that's taking place with the individual in the realm of the Mind—has all this emotional encoding and imprinting and energy attached to it as a mass at a lower level.

And so, the individual is constantly—they're trying to think rationally and function and, you know, commanding the "Mind–Body" system from *Self*, but there's all these—all this other information is being thrown on the line; erroneous information is being stirred up that has nothing to do with Self-determination, meaning nothing to do with *Self* determining its own experience.

Basically, emotional fragmentation in beta-existence means: instead of getting a clear view of what is taking place around in the environment, all of these other mechanisms are sending all these other signals about anything that could be associated with that.

It's basically for this reason that many attempts—the "light work," the "New Age healing" methods and some of that—have not proven to be as effective among some practitioners as perhaps they could be. The main reason because the ZU-energy is a constant—it's coming in at a constant—and we're dealing with these imprints and programming and masses and mechanizations that really just weren't understood "systematically" *from* the mystical perspective.

Just like, you know, the "chakra-alignment" puts us in check today; tomorrow the individual—their uncorrected mode of thought and the way it's associated to various emotional levels and the type of energy processing taking place as a result—it's just gonna put them back into the same situation tomorrow.

The individual is really responsible for being able to manage their own direction of Self-determinism—as the Mind or as even the emotional reactivity—being able to observe and command emotional reactivity. Otherwise, the individual *as Self* is basically going more and more into the realm of "effect."

And so, I mean—really, when you consider even the "mental healing practices" or the "faith healing practices" and some of these other "spiritual" and "New Age" methodologies, we're really talking about the treatment of the *individual*, and getting the *individual* to a point where *they* are basically able to handle the *body* themselves. They are the ones essentially healing the body; the physician is basically there only as an *assistant* to *that*. That's something that even some of the higher minds in the medical field today even know—this is not something we are just now "cooking up."

It's ironic because the principles of Systemology, for example, as relayed in "*The Tablets of Destiny*" text, they're not in contradiction, really, with medical knowledge. I mean, they just—some individuals though—they just no longer see the Human Condition or the Spirit for what it is, because their science is: fragmenting to analyze only one part in exclusion to all others. This just puts in more and more considerations that the individual is *only* the physical condition—and treating only the physical levels.

I mean, *that's* a perfect example of someone being fixed in only a certain mode of Awareness—but, you know, on an intellectual level. It's somewhat different than the type of "programming" you see in emotionally encoded imprints, but once a *belief* is imprinted, it's continually reinforced with emotional energy through the validation of the experience—using that as a *filter* of experience, and with that experience, basically validating and reinforcing the *filter* and strengthening the *filter*.

When we talk about "beta-defragmentation," we're talking about getting an individual into a greater point of *cause* as opposed to *effect*—even in terms of the responsibility of their own Mind, of their memory, of the emotional imprinting and "conditioning" that has been, essentially, attached to that associative knowledge in their own mind. This is up to an individual to handle.

In most cases, emotional imprinting and such—the type of heavy fragmentation that's been taking place—for example, in an individual's *current* lifetime, it's not usually the result of something they're doing to themselves, but something that others that have done to them. So, to spend a lot of time validating this, for example, with some of the "*cathartic processing*" methods—"Route-1"—as it's treated...

The method that is given at the very end of "*The Tablets of Destiny*" text is called "Route-1" once we get into higher levels of Systemology, and it's the "*cathartic processing*" method—and this can be used, essentially, to help an individual overcome the point of "*shock*" that takes place when this imprint is kind of snapped like a camera shutter. It's very effective if you're treating something that's happened to an individual relatively recently. This is one way in which Mardukite Ministers can actually apply Systemology to *assist* those that are coming to them.

But when it's used as the *only* method of treating imprinting or what's taken place and the *only* processing route, it actually has a tendency to *validate* or *strengthen* the idea that an individual is operating with the "Reactive Control Center" in exclusion to any other command of the Mind.

And so, really, the idea behind "*cathartic processing*"—or "abbreactive processing" as some of the early psychologist and psychoanalysists were experimenting with it in the early 1900's—this is a form of "*regression therapy*" actually. Although it's effective, it can be even in some ways be administered by Self—because we can spot and scan through these events and handle them *if* they're within our ability to *handle*.

The reason that we kind of employ *Piloting*—Professional Piloting—in our Mardukite Systemology and the advanced levels that even Mardukite Ministers can reach—in terms of training and education and the application of this—is because most of the time *if* an individual *was* able, if these "traditional Self-Help books" and the methods have been employed for, you know, countless decades now and ever since "New Thought," were effective as they could be... I mean, there's nothing wrong with the information necessarily, but then we're leaving it up to the individual to not only *process* this information out of books on their own, but then *duplicate* the understanding of the authors and then also their methods in achieving various things.

That leaves a lot up to "chance"—that puts a lot on someone to have to basically "get right" during their lifetime, with hits and misses. But, with Professional Piloting—which is something that we deal with beyond the Mardukite Master Course—but, Professional Piloting: the application of these principles to assist our fellow man in structured systematic way—it has been proven effective; even more effective than, again, what some individuals have been able to achieve on their own, even using these same materials and techniques.

Now, that's one reason why I *did* establish a "self-processing" methodology in the *"Crystal Clear"* volume. *"The Tablets of Destiny"* and *"Crystal Clear"* basically compose the entirety of what we deal with concerning the actual standard for Grade-III. Now, there's other texts within *"The Systemology Handbook"* such as *"Systemology: The Original Thesis"* and *"The Power of Zu"* and some of these supplemental outlines and so forth—they're simply there because we're dealing with a Master-level understanding of how we developed this work and what we're doing with it.

And so, on an outer level, *"The Tablets of Destiny"* was really the founding text—the main core text—of Grade-III Mardukite Systemology; and then in order to make the Grade *effective*—in order to actually achieve the goals and ideals that are reflective *of* the "Third Gate," the Third Grade, we had to develop a "self-processing" manual, which is called *"Crystal Clear,"* which can be used by an individual *or even* as a Professional Piloting manual to assist the procedures.

: LECTURE 45—CRYSTAL CLEAR :
(September 30, 2020)

[Alright, here we are on the last day of the Mardukite Master Course. You've, uh, you've made it all this far. We didn't lose any one—we had some visitors on the way; but we didn't lose anyone that had set out to get through this course. This is the forty-fifth lecture of the Mardukite Master Course, the final day that we're doing lectures—the final lectures of the course. I believe it's September 30, 2020—and we've done just about everything now but actually cover and discuss the most recent work, the capstone of the Mardukite Master Grades—the final book that essentially capped off what we treat as Grade-III, which is Mardukite Systemology.]

So, the final book that capped off this Grade came out—it was released actually to the public less than a year ago; and it's (public) title is *"Crystal Clear"*—that's Mardukite Systemology *"Liber-2B."* And this is the practical companion to *"The Tablets of Destiny"* material, which was released only a couple of months prior to *that*. And the combination of those two—all of that material, of course, being in *"The Systemology Handbook,"* our Grade-III textbook for the Mardukite Master Course—this essentially brought us to the point of... well, brought *me* to a point, because this was essentially a personal endeavor that was finally effective enough to deliver to others.

I mean, spanning a quarter-of-a-century, with an academic background in "psychology," "magick and metaphysics," "Druidism," establishment of the "Mardukites," the institutionalization of a *new* systematic study—or a way, or a paradigm—a more holistic paradigm of which to view the world as systemology... I was finally actually about to do what I had wanted to do *[laughs]* when I was a teenager, which was to write the definitive "Self-Help" book.

I had read so many of them—been inspired by so many of them. When this all first began in the 1990's, I would go out to—when I was in high school still; when I was in the formative time for developing "Elven Fellowship Circle of Magick"—I would go out; we had an open campus during high school; the high school I was attending during the development of all this in the 1990's—because I talk about how much was going on with me in the 1990's and so forth—well, we has an open campus and our high school was directly across the street from Washington Park in Denver, which is the largest park in the Denver.

It's not as large as Central Park (in New York) or Golden Gate Park in San Francisco, but it's similar—it's in the middle of the city, and it's just this long rectangle of trailways and trees and two lakes in it and so forth.

So, every lunch period I would go out—we had an hour for lunch—and I would go out and meet with people; and eventually it turned into meeting as a "*coven*" and as the "*Elven Fellowship Circle*," but in the beginning, I would just go out and stand on this bench and I would start reading "*The Way of the Wizard*" by Deepak Chopra—and I would start reading the chapters and stories from it, read his discussions and so forth.

Those that were there—I mean, at first, there was only a couple people that were there. But, we had, at one point, there were several dozen people all surrounding me while I was reading from this book. And afterward, there would be like a short period of time for discussion and so forth; and this is actually what ended up leading to the membership that composed the "Elven Fellowship Circle" and others that I was reaching.

I mean, I went to a high school that had *1,600* students, so I was able to reach at least a specific target demographic from that—and we would meet in Washington Park; and this was during the time period when I was also going out to the

Metaphysical Bookstores, but yeah, I was just a teenager.

I was working on all these works as "Merlyn Stone"—I would bring copies of the "*Sorcerer's Handbook*" and various works and, you know, would sell them to these stores and get them to start helping establish [*laughs*] this underground presence of mine.

At that time, again, I was working under the name of "Merlyn Stone" and then I started writing under various other names too—doing all kinds of various work—just basically trying to *do* the work; I wasn't really establishing myself as "Joshua Free" at that time.

The other point being that I was working on a lot of this while still in high school; and one of the things that happened—there were several times when I was actually pulled into the Office and they would this copy of "*The Sorcerer's Handbook*" sitting there and they would actually like pressure me to tell them like—they said they knew about the "coven" that was operating in their school and they wanted to know about the other members and, I mean, I wouldn't give them anything.

I was kind of a rebel in high school. It's kind of hard to categorize me—we didn't have a "goth wall" or anything like that; it was pretty much *just me*, weird outlandish me, kinda running around [*laughs*] and doing all kinds of various stuff. And then at the same time, I had mentioned in a *previous* lecture about when I was a guest speaker in several of my classes in high school—one of them being "psychology."

I had given several classes on "psychology" in the 1990's, mainly pertaining to "Carl Jung" and "Timothy Leary"—and of course, the school board was aware of that as well; and of course, I wasn't really hiding some of my [*dramatically clears throat*] pursuits and such, at the time, you know, things that I've explored and since gone beyond—I don't really condone much of it; there are of course, these higher ways of understanding and examining things, but I don't begrudge anyone their own experiences or their own path to figure things out for themselves.

I believe that we can establish a higher pinnacle of effective results and really a higher quality standard for Actualization and personal development within our Systemology and leading people to that with Mardukite Zuism, far greater than promising Ascension at five bucks a *hit*.

It doesn't really work "across the board" and so, what I've really focused on now rather than "altered states of consciousness" and some underground pursuits that I was dealing with for probably the first decade that I was exploring some of this information and some of this stuff that I now relay on a more "metaphysical" level or in more academic scholarly writings.

Basically, *"Crystal Clear"* demonstrates the pinnacle of Grade-III Mardukite Systemology. And although it has since been pulled in for incorporation into Piloted work and higher grades of Systemology and kind of what we're doing and delivering in that aspect—but again, in the Mardukite Master Course we're primarily concerned with these first three Grades as "Knowledge Grades." That's not to say that there isn't "practical tech" to be found throughout the whole journey of it.

However, my emphasis in talking about *"Crystal Clear"* today, is referring to it as it was originally intended, which is essentially a *Self-Help* book—to replace all those that came before it that turned out to be *No-Help* books. And it's actually even been pointed out to me how much "esoteric" and "high-level" work—Master-level work—is actually incorporated into *"Crystal Clear"* in spite of it being presented in kind of this more "psychology/self-help/self-improvement/awareness"-type material— very different from the other kinds of work that I've done, which seem to be geared toward a more specific "occult" or "esoteric" paradigm.

And yet, by background and such, my delivery in this—and the goals that I had set forth—I mean, this wasn't just to write another book. There had been goals set forth each step of the way—and the presentation of "*Crystal Clear*" was basically... Well, just as much as "*The Original Thesis*" and all of the work that went into the backbone and the forgotten history and legacy [*laughs*] of our efforts in Systemology—that kind of developed into "*The Tablets of Destiny.*"

And then the companion work for that—that was released in the underground as "*Reality Engineering*"—I was able to take the elements of that and really bring a much clearer understanding and an actual practical methodology of development; because, a lot of these premises were already put forth nearly a decade ago. I started giving the "*Reality Engineering*" lectures back in 2008 and 2009; and kind of did that in the background of all the Mardukite work that was going on at the time, for those that were interested.

Then, I started developing, the materials for "*The Original Thesis*" in 2010 and 2011, when I was wrapping up my work for the "Mardukite Core." And in 2013, I found myself living primarily alone in California—well, I was living with an artist at the time—living alone in California and examining all the work that had brought me to that point.

And this was after—I had talked about the "Games" and stuff *yesterday* in one of our *previous* lectures—and I was basically in a reflection-point; and I was looking at my notes from over the course... everything that hadn't been developed yet beyond Grade-II Mardukite work; and I started to compile them into what became the "*Reality Engineering*" release.

Now, honestly—to be completely honest with you—only a few dozen people really ever acquired "*Reality Engineering*" at the time; and it kind of went over a lot of people's heads. It was really meant to deliver the *next step beyond* the outlines in, for example, "*The Original Thesis*" material. It...

I mean, many of the concepts appear in our Systemology from *"Reality Engineering"* in those previous forms. We've changed some of the semantics—we've refined some of the understanding—but one can see, I mean, this isn't something that just kind of churned up overnight, even though the material for Systemology is now being developed, published and delivered at kind of an exponential rate.

The slower beginnings of this are still set down there. And in the appendix to *"The Systemology Handbook"*—and actually also with the *"Mardukite Master Course: Instructor's Manual"*— you will find a very comprehensive outline for the delivery of the *"Reality Engineering"* lectures—which was considered "Systemology 2.0" because prior to being released as it's current form as *"The Original Thesis,"* all of those booklets that had composed it, had been put together in an anthology edition titled *"Systemology 101: The Awakening"* and that was considered "Systemology 1.0"; and *"Reality Engineering"* was considered "Systemology 2.0."

We kind of followed in the same spirit of that, where I was able to revitalize the concepts of *"The Original Thesis"* in relation to cuneiform tablets for *"The Tablets of Destiny"* and create a more cohesive bridge between the Mardukite work and Systemology; because, honestly back in 2011-12-13—although if you read *"Liber-R"* in the Grade-II work, you'll see that this is where it was obviously progressing at the end of the Mardukite Core; and if you look at *"Arcanum"* and you look at some of the "Druidism" as it's presented in *"Merlyn's Complete Book of Druidism,"* you'll see that this was always the upper-level goals; this wasn't something that just emerged out of nowhere.

But it took some time in the refinement and development of that which came before it—what we treat as Grade-I and Grade-II—in order to really present Mardukite Systemology, which is simply the name given to this "paradigm" that I was able to establish over the last twenty-five years; this unique approach to not only everything that we've covered in the Mardukite Master Course, but also everything that we're going to now—everything that we're moving towards.

Now with the completion of Grade-III, I was able to start focusing on Grade-IV. And the first components of that are soon to be released—well, they're released in the underground—but are soon to be released as *"Metahuman Destinations: Piloting the Course to Homo Novus."*

And so, we've achieved specific goals with *"Crystal Clear"* and we're incorporating that; it doesn't become an obsolete book once you get to Grade-IV.

It doesn't become obsolete; it simply represents particular goals reached, for example, Grade-III and its delivery—and what it's able to achieve. *"Crystal Clear."* We have individuals —it's been released almost a year ago—and we have individuals that have been using it *daily*, adamantly using it and applying it continuously, even though they've reached many of the pinnacle points within that material. So, they continue to use that *and* it is, again, an incredible *tool* for an individual to have for themselves, assuming they don't have access to Professional Piloting or other mentorships regarding this information.

This is something that you could easily gift somebody and it would improve their life; it really would. I stand behind—I mean, we are still ironing out the *higher-level* ideals and aspirations and goals; but, when it comes to what I've spent, really since my aspirations as a teenager twenty-five years ago to develop a place in the underground and trying to push more into the mainstream with our work—it's an achievement of goals; goals completed. And so, that's what we are representing in the Mardukite Master Course.

So now, I want to spend the rest of the day talking about the material in *"Crystal Clear,"* because if we're talking about a Master-level understanding, and we're talking about a Master Course—and we're talking about a level of Mastery concerning all of the materials that have been developed up to this point—the pinnacle and what we...

Well, although we're talking about a Master-level of understanding and the ability for you as an Instructor or Mentor or various groups or franchising a lodge or something within the Mardukite tradition, we're talking about a Master-level or a Master Course being the Master Grades. The "Master Grades" were supposed to entail "getting to the point" of *Crystal Clear*—what the material is describing in *that text*.

And so, while we consider Grade-I as *one of* the "Master Grades" and Grade-II as *one of* the "Master Grades," what is actually defining the "Mardukite Master Course"—or the Master understanding or the Master-level—of *this* Systemology *is* essentially explored *at* Grade-III. And so, we spent some significant time going through that—giving a clear understanding of all that—that you will be able to carry with and duplicate in, not only your own personal life, but also in your deliver of this.

That's why—and I've said it a couple times now—it's a little bit exciting for me to be able to deliver this part of, for example, the Mardukite Master Course above the others, which I have covered previously—which I've spent considerably more time working with people with in the past. Whereas, for example, talking about "*Crystal Clear*," other than the lectures given during the development of the book, the only other time I've really talked about it—because everything I've been doing this year has been related to Grade-IV and also the establishment of Mardukite Zuism as a "religious division" of our work.

But other than "*The Power of Zu*"—and the lecture transcripts from that from a year ago are found in the appendix of "*The Systemology Handbook*" and the "*Instructor's Manual*"—but other than that point, I've never, for almost a year now, I've not really delivered any kind of overviews; I haven't really been introducing any new people to this; I haven't been giving an overlay of the material.

So, this is the first time we are doing that; and in the past, we haven't even been *recording them* for distribution—we've been basically been recording them so that I could apply transcripts from the workshops and experimental periods with the books, with the actual book releases.

You'll notice there are transcripts in the original edition of "*The Tablets of Destiny*," which I have a feeling will be revised in how it's presented—but, the original edition of "*The Tablets of Destiny*" still being used, and that edition used to compose the Master Edition of the Grade-III work in "*The Systemology Handbook.*" So, *that* will never change, in terms of what the original relay of that material was or the original edition.

We've been focusing on both the Mardukite Academy of Systemology and also the Church of Mardukite Zuism as essentially the two ongoing factions of the original Mardukite Ministries (Mardukite Umbrella). And so, the recent release of the "*Anunnaki Bible: New Standard Zuist Edition*," it's the premiere edition representing—although the Joshua Free Imprint published it—it's the premiere edition representing the Church of Mardukite Zuism; so that's the first edition of material presented *specifically* as a Church of Mardukite Zuism presentation.

When we release newer editions down the road as Mardukite Academy volumes, this will be when, either we retain the information as it exists at a Master-level or treat, for example, simplicities of it—for example, as an abridged version, the way that "*Anunnaki Bible: New Standard Zuist Edition*" is, so that from the religious—from the entry level stand point—for example, coming from Grade-II or treating Mardukite Zuism as a modern religion—or Mesopotamian Neopaganism—we have an ability to kind of abridge and simplify an entry point into these higher levels of learning and understanding.

It's not that there's anything inherently *wrong* with our original presentations of work, but what most of you have observed and experienced—if you've been around over the past decade or so—is that it's really gone through a period of refinements; and we've been able to reach that pinnacle, for example, all the materials of the Mardukite Master Course—we've been able to reach that pinnacle now, in the way of refinement and delivery in a way we have not been able to accomplish before.

My goals in deliver things though—when we talk about *"Crystal Clear"*—we're not going to talk about it in the way that I would in a "Flight School" or in a Piloting Course. I want to talk to you about *"Crystal Clear"* as it was originally intended—as a "self-help" book for *you*; *you* being the Master.

This course is, of course, intended for *you*—but on that note, what it represents is that those that are able to complete course, those that are able to actually work through the materials of the Mardukite Master Course, work from all the volumes regardless of what editions you have—that's one of the reasons we prepared the *"Instructor's Manual,"* because the *"Instructor's Manual"* for the Mardukite Master Course is composed of the appendices that have been attached to each of the Master Editions.

So, if you have all of the material that appears in, for example, "Necronomicon: The Complete Anunnaki Legacy" from former editions—the only difference being, for the new Master Edition, that we have this "Appendix" of various Master Course outlines and background information, and so forth, that ties everything together.

And so, for those that have all the materials in the former editions that have been collected over the years—and aren't necessarily ready, or in a position, to upgrade their collection or their library with the new anthology textbooks, the *"Mardukite Master Course Instructor's Manual"* is essentially all of the appendices that have been attached to that, so that basically you'll still have the complete information. And then in addition to this, down the road, we'll of course release the "transcripts" for the lectures. When we consider transcripts to *48 lectures* combined, I'm sure that will be a hefty volume in itself.

Now, the original edition of *"Crystal Clear"*—and as it appears in *"The Systemology Handbook"*—is introduced by Kyra Kaos; and although most people only know of Kyra Kaos as the graphics manager for the Joshua Free Imprint, she's been responsible for the state of all the new cover designs since 2018, where we've been reintroducing all of the texts that were formerly published underground, now under the Joshua Free Imprint.

And she is—what many don't know know—she's also been responsible for the assistance of development at the Systemology Society of the Systemology work for now almost two years, ever since I began putting my emphasis back onto it. I decided in 2018, when a lot of the original discoveries for *"The Tablets of Destiny"* were being made, that this was the direction that I needed to be focused on; and by putting that determination in, I was able to finally reach the pinnacle of Grade-III work and deliver what is now all the material in *"The Systemology Handbook"* and the various books composing that anthology.

Now, *"Crystal Clear"*—the work of *"Crystal Clear"* and the program I established for that—it *did* assume that an individual probably had already read *"The Tablets of Destiny"* and so had some basic familiarity with what we were dealing with. Of course, this wasn't absolutely necessary in order to get effective results from the work.

The first *challenge*, once I had established the work and knew that it was completed—had applied it to *myself*—was to establish a *standard evaluation* of actually charting the progress that one was going to be encountering while working through the new Grade-III Mardukite Systemology.

So, I established what was called the "BAT" [*laughs*]—a lot of this work was being developed as we were coming up to Halloween and so that came into play multiple times—but, it's the *"Beta Awareness Test,"* and this was developed to determine a basic or average state of personal awareness; particularly *"beta-Awareness"* or what was maintained by an individual—the Alpha Spirit—as they were managing the genetic vehicle to have the experience of the Human Condition in beta-existence.

So, we had to some up with a system of evaluation and assessment. I had a background in psychology—had taken countless tests myself. Although some say that this could have been simplified even more—or why did I make it so hard [*laughs*] in terms of calculating and charting it; this is really the most complex—the *minimal* amount of complexity that was necessary to chart and access information that I wanted to get from it.

Is it perfect? No. *Hell, no.* But... is it effective? Oh, yes. It is an effective benchmark in establishing and charting one's increase in beta-Awareness; it is effective for that.

An individual is asked to, essentially, answer—with an assessment scale of "0" being "never" and "4" being "always" —and there's *blanks* in each statement; for example, "I *blank* take care of, maintain and treat my physical environment well"; and then there's an *assessment scale*: "never," "rarely," "sometimes," "usually," "very often," "consistently" and "always"—and there are certain numbers that are attached to those.

When you go through, each question—basically, for example, there's "Question A-5" or "Question J-6" and so forth. Each of those "letters" represents a particular subject or component; and so what we have is, basically, six questions analyzing a particular facet or component of the Human experience.

There's *one-hundred* questions total; and the reason I did this was because it was easiest to establish an "average" and so forth—moving decimal points around once you total it. And you don't really need to know a whole lot of "math"—there's instructions about how to put it into this "graph" and "table" and essentially just add up various answers and get the results.

There's various things that are treated in this. For example, all the questions—D-1 and D-2 and D-3 (up to six) all concern managing external reality in one's environment. Another one—like, all the "N" questions are about managing personal tolerance to others.

What you do is—you're basically adding up and figuring out in each one of these areas, this score between "0" and "4"; and then you're treating the entire total as an average—and that comes, you know, you end up reducing that value to a point between "0" and "4" and what you end up basically getting—and we've talking about the Standard Model a bit—you're basically able to put an individual, position them, on the Standard Model concerning the ZU-line. And, for example, when we were talking about the extension of "*Reality Engineering*"—and in "Reality Engineering" nearly a decade ago, we were simply calling (the ZU-line) the "Personal Identity Continuum" and, of course, that's a mouthful; so, now we're calling it the "ZU-line."

We've talked about "0" to "4" basically being the *interior* components of the Mind-System and being *internal* to the experience of the Human Condition as beta-Awareness within beta-existence—within the Physical Universe. You can actually determine, kind of, a "benchmark" within that range of where an individual *is*; and of course, we have classifications assigned to all of the numeric values possible.

And those classifications were simplified into the "Emotimeter"—which is what we are referring to it as, which basically gave the general, for example, "0.5" "1" "1.5" "2" "2.5" and so on—just the general states that one might be fixing *Beingness*, fixing their *point-of-view*, along the ZU-line.

And then with the full "Beta-Awareness Scale" we were able to pull that apart even more. I mean, I was using—I was pulling out all kinds of "psychology" textbooks and "Self-Help" books and various "New Thought" and "creative psychology" manuals from the 1950's and 1960's and trying to distinguish all the different *points* that an individual could have and be experiencing.

I mean, we came up *forty-two* different frequencies or degrees of the ZU-line concerning "thought" and "emotion." [*Laughs*] So, we established the "Beta-Awareness Scale" and aligned it with the "Standard Model" and the experience of the Human Condition, so that we could actually apply these key words—whether it was being "afraid" or being "evasive" or being "dismissive" or being "interested" or "enthusiastic"—all these different things we could chart now as various levels of beta-Awareness on the ZU-line.

And this is one of the amazing breakthroughs that I had made with working on the material for "*The Tablets of Destiny*"—but, again, a lot of this ended up being finally delivered... Basically, the culmination of [*laughs*] all the work I had spent so much time trying to *get to*, was finally delivered with the "*Crystal Clear*" manual.

Also, it became clear that—when we we're talking about the basic needs and beta-dynamics of "survival" concerning the Human Condition—that we we're running very parallel with Abraham Maslow's "Pyramid of Self-Actualization," which suited my purposes just fine, because, you know, "actualization" is the intent behind all of this.

So, at "1," you've got Self, the physiology of the genetic vehicle, primitive survival; at "2," you have the family unit, domestic security; at "3," you have group interactions, the establishment of purpose, carrying out goals, thinking things through and carrying out to achieve those; and then at "4," you have all humanity, success and personal esteem.

These were the basis of Abraham Maslow's "Pyramid" and yet, we were also finding, again, what we were presenting as "Spheres of Influence"—the "Spheres of Existence"—between Self at "1" and, you know, the home and domestic situation at "2," involvement with groups at "3," and then all of humanity at "4"—and then basically defining all of the parameters of the Human Condition as a genetic vehicle, beta-existence, sensory-awareness, emotion, thought and so forth at "4."

And, of course, we were talking about—on the Standard Model—you know, the "MCC" and "RCC"... All of this was coming together finally. So, as I say, "*Crystal Clear*" was this brilliant culmination of all the work and all the various facets that I had been piecing together throughout the years, and almost just like carrying little "napkin notes" around with—and going, "Well, *one day* all this will come into place and fix together and we'll be able to establish this." [*Laughs*]

So, in essence, when we're talking about "Self-Evaluation," we're talking about simply the ability—and we're not comparing to other people; we're not putting unrealistic goals in front of us—we're simply trying to demonstrate; because you can use the numeric values from the "Beta-Awareness Test" and then, kind of, evaluate yourself, as far as *seeing* visible some representation—although I'm sure you'll experience it—but seeing it graphically; we've been able to demonstrate.

Because, again, we're treating this just a little bit more "scientifically" and a little less, you know, "superficially" in trying to at least *gauge* something; seeing that two weeks and four weeks and, you know, several months and so forth of working with this material would actually create a visible *change* on something that we could chart—with the standard of the "Beta-Awareness Test."

And so, the introduction of "*Crystal Clear*"—before it starts getting into really any of the "Awareness Tech" and "Actualization" and trying to get an individual, through "beta-defragmentation"—it basically introduces this model of the "Beta-Awareness Scale," the "Beta-Awareness Test."

This same test and all the—you know, if an individual doesn't want to mark up their textbook or their copy of this—the tests and charts and all of the stuff that you might be "logging" or rather, keeping a "journal" of as you progress through this, is also available—and we have a publication from the Systemology Society that's called "*Systemology: Pathway to Self-Honesty Truth Seeker's Adventure Journal.*" And this is a very inexpensive, specially designed, notebook that allows you to keep track of all this stuff and record all this stuff—including your "self-processing" or even "Piloted Processing"—all within this journal.

So, that is another tool—although it's... I believe, in your "*Instructor's Manual*," there's information about "logging" the processing sessions and so forth; but, really, we have this entire "Adventure Journal"—is what we refer to it as—that an individual can actually keep track of all this; and actually even retain multiple copies of it, very inexpensively, to chart their progress on the *Pathway to Self-Honesty*—and beyond to the *Gateways of Infinity*.

: LECTURE 46—AWARENESS TECH :
(September 30, 2020)

Now, after Self-Evaluation—if you're following along in "*Crystal Clear*"; and we'll try to stick to the way it's presented, because there's no "outline" for "*Liber-2B*," which is the designation for "*Crystal Clear.*" There's no outline for this given; this, again, is the most recent development concerning the *twenty-five* years that's going into the materials of the Mardukite Master Course.

These materials do not become obsolete later on. We refer to "*The Tablets of Destiny*" and "*Crystal Clear*" constantly, in regards to my work at Grade-IV. And it's not that Grade-IV is "oh, so much higher" than this; but we're dealing with, again, another level of understanding above it—and taking its applications higher.

We're still working on standardization of "Mardukite Systemology" in the Systemology Society; we're working on the establishment of all of the ways in which "Piloting" can be delivered—and also instructed—all of that aspect is still in development. What *has* been established, is the first three "Grades" that compose the entirety of the Master-levels or "Master Grades"—the Mardukite Master Course.

And we've been treating these *other* "Grades"—these *higher-level* "Grades"—as "Wizard Grades" or "Actualized Technician Grades" or "A.T. Grades." And not because we're trying to "hide" something or because an individual needs to somehow get new specialized "initiation" or something into some "secret" level of learning—it's just, again, the "Master-level" of understanding that I was after, regarding the "Master-level" of, for example, the project of mine, "*Hermetic Order of the Crystal Dawn*" back in the 1990's—which was one of the conceptions of my "Merlyn School."

So, the idea was that we would be treating this stuff—at these various gradients and levels of initiation and, basically, instruction and personal exploration—reaching the point of a "Master." And, so, it's literally taken, even myself, *twenty-five* years to do that in a way that I was confident behind what that term and that level of understanding and that "Grade" of knowledge and practice actually represented; because, you know, *anyone* can just throw around the word "Master" or so forth. I had particular goals in mind, which were reached.

So, in following along—once we deal with "Self-Evaluation," the next determinant factor of "*Crystal Clear*" deals with Awareness. And so, I introduce in the text, the "*Beta-Awareness Scale*"—the full "Awareness Scale" as a means to, you know... And this isn't to, like, belittle someone—as far as plotting them from the "*Beta-Awareness Test*" or anything like that. The intention behind it is simply to show just a baseline of where an individual is at as a chronic state.

Obviously, an individual has different levels of *attention* or *interest* attached to various subjects—and with emotional encoding, well, obviously, an individual has various levels of emotional reaction to different things; but what the "*Beta-Awareness Test*" was intended—what the "BAT" test is intended to do—is simply gauge a "chronic" state of where an individual is at in maintaining a Self-determined Human experience.

The other purpose, again, being that I've been looking at various ways of "spiritual advisement" and "counseling" and so forth for multiple decades, and so behind this—the "hidden tech" behind this, I guess, when you're talking about upper-level Piloting—it was a way to also gauge "Session Awareness" and gauge where an individual is at regarding a particular *facet* or particular *subject.*

And so we gauge these things; we talked a little bit about this in the *last* lecture—but we gauge these things. Up from, for example, almost like "death" at "0" to all through the idea of "victimization" and "hopelessness" and "depression" and "suffering" at "0.5"; and then "grief" and "terror" and "resentment" and "anxiety" and all that around the fear level of "1"; and then the outright "confrontational," "violent," "hatefulness," "rage" and "anger" at "1.5."

The "antagonistic," also the level of "pain," "monotonous" —you know, this kind of "invalidating"—almost near "indifference" we find at "2"; and then at "2.0" we also have our "Reactive Control Center." So, basically, on the "Beta-Awareness Scale" and in regards to the Standard Model, at "2.0" we have the "Reactive Control Center," which basically kicks in some kind of emotional response regarding all of those conditions that I just described.

And then above, "2.0"—for example, the "indifference" or, you know, "bored" and so forth at "2.5"; and then above that we have any kind of "interest" being applied, "mild interests" and "strong interests" and all that around the "3.0" level. "Determinant," "eagerness" and "cheerfulness" and so forth, around "3.5"; and then, of course, we're talking, you know; when we're talking about this kind of state of generalized "Beta-Awareness," where we're talking about "actualization"—"beta-Actualization" or "beta-defragmentation"—we're talking about the "Master Control Center"; a perfected clear channel between the experience of *Self* and the command of the *body* at the "Master Control Center," which is at "4.0."

Although we're not—well, the idea behind the "Beta-Awareness Test" and the idea behind Grade-III and "*Crystal Clear*," I should point out—is not to necessarily "*score*" "4.0" on all the tests and so forth, because that's not what this is a reflection of. When we're talking about total "defragmentation" and every circuit and every aspect that could somehow impinge itself on the Human experience, we're dealing at "upper-level" stuff—stuff that we start dealing more with at the "Wizard Grades" because that's when, based on this foundation, I was able to actually tear things apart deeper. That's the work I've been doing this year in 2020.

But, when we're talking about the "Master Course" of everything from 1995 up *until* "this," than yeah: "*Crystal Clear*" is the epitome and basically the defining information and knowledge level of what we want to treat as a Master Grade.

So, the functional element behind "*Crystal Clear*" is what has developed as "self-processing." *Processing*—I talked about in a *former* lecture when we were talking about a "function machine." We were talking about, as an example, this idea that you enter something in this "box" or this "machine" or the "Human Condition" or its wiring—for example, the Mind-System *processes* it a certain way and then it yields a certain result, which would be the information or experience the Self is essentially getting from this.

The idea of *processing*—that's what we mean by that. The reason that I've started emphasizing this idea of "processing"—*procedures* of "processing," "piloted processing," "self-processing"—is because... I want to make sure it's clear... There's all kinds of information in your textbook and in "*Crystal Clear*" about what "self-processing" *is*; the biggest —the thing I want to point out *here*, is more to the point of what it *isn't*.

For example, it's *not* "meditation." Now, yes, an individual is meant to be "grounded" when their practicing this; but, this isn't a "blank out" of, you know, "focus on nothing," spend an hour "sitting and breathing" in a certain position and basically, you know, "think of nothing"—or *try* to "focus on nothing" or "concentrate on nothing" or whatever "meditation" means to you in that respect; it's *not* that. It's *not* really "prayer"—we're not necessarily trying to communicate with something *outside* of ourselves; we're not trying to communicate with the "Source" or the "Divine" or the "Other" or anything of that respect; it's *not* that.

It's *not* personal "Self-talk"—it's not the type of "voices" or "circuit-voices" that you have running in your head; or the dialogue that you'll often exchange with yourself and be actually engaging with other "voices" or "personalities" or whatever—that seem like entities; these other kind of things... it's *not* that.

And it's *not* "freewheeling"—it's not the kind of "random thought" or "light recall" you might do in just like occupying normative existence, where everything and anything that attracts your attention could trigger some kind of associative idea or concept or so on and so forth. So, those are all the things that "Systemology Processing" is *not*.

What I kind of like to think of it as—and this may be more (accurately) a point where an individual is working through "*Wizard Levels*," but—*solo-piloting*, where you are expertly applying the aspects of "Systemology Processing" without the aid of another *Pilot*, or even another "friend" or so forth to read the questions or whatnot out loud.

Because that's another possible component: prior to any kind of "Piloting" aspects that we start to deal with at Grade-IV, the real experiment—the proof behind it—was that this was being done with just "regular" individuals without that kind of expert level "pilot" knowledge—and by that I mean: the delivery of this information; the execution of the "processing" in a particular systematic session format. So, we weren't doing any of that back in Grade-III *anyways*—we were just applying the basic concepts and [*laughs*] finding that there were effective results from that.

The other purpose of the "Beta Awareness Scale" and gauging the levels of emotional reactivity and thought and so forth, is that regardless of what an individual's "chronic" level is—regardless of what they might be carrying themselves as at any given point—there's also the level that is brought when the "Reactive Control Center" is kicked it.

Now, it may be that a person's "chronic" state *is* below "2.0" *because* that's the condition that they're in. They're currently engaged primarily in an emotional state, because whether something has recently happened to them—or some kind of trauma has held along with them.

But, most of the time, an individual will be found on the "Beta-Awareness Test" above "2.0." In fact, you really don't want to engage in any kind of processing *below* that, in terms of what we're treating in "*Crystal Clear*," which at higher-levels—for example, the methodology of "*The Tablets of Destiny*" is treated as "Route-1" and the methodology of "*Crystal Clear*" is referred to as "Route-2" *when* you start to deal with upper-level "Piloting" and it's systematic cataloging and designation of all these techniques.

"Route-1" is kind of emotional... reducing the emotional charge on something, or assisting an individual with what they're dealing with at that moment—because they're not ready to sit down and start thinking about things and analyzing things; they're already *restimulated* into a point where they're engaging with the environment as a danger, for whatever reasons—whatever imprinting has been done.

And so, for example, there you have a differentiation between what we treat in "Mardukite Zuism" as the level of assistance and basic counseling that, for example, a Mardukite Minister would provide in, kind of, these emergency situations—or basically to get an individual *out of* this, like, clear and present emotional reactive state; because that's what they're dealing with at that time.

When we start to talk about the Systemology Society and we're talking about "Professional Piloting," we're no longer dealing with, necessarily, the Mardukite Zuist "religion" or the basic spiritual aid that's delivered by a Minister—we're talking about a more advanced form of "piloted" assistance and counseling and spiritual advisement that is—again, this is something we're going to have individuals *trained* for.

And the Mardukite Master Course is able to allow you to have an understanding of all these concepts—all these materials—throughout the three Grades; and even be able to instruct in them, in not only your own schools and academy divisions and various lodges and groups—but, when it comes to this "upper-level" application of specifically the "Systemology Procedures" and "Systematic Processing"— we're talking about another caliber altogether.

So, that's why, honestly, what we're going to end up doing is: we have the Mardukite Master Course for the "instructive" levels and to give an individual their *own* sense of "Mastery" over the materials—and then, we plan on having the Mardukite Ministers of the Church of Mardukite Zuism have *their* own course in administrating and the type of work that goes into being "clergy" and the Mardukite "religion" and its standards—and then separately from that, the Systemology Society dealing with the "piloting" and the more advanced levels of this philosophy as an "applied spiritual technology."

In a *previous* lecture, I was talking about *facets*; I was talking about the ability to deal with the events that have emotional encoding with them and imprinting and the ability to resurface them—and by going through them multiple times, having an individual, in a point of Self-determination, in a point of intentional application of attention and awareness, *be able* to actually reduce the emotional charge that takes place on the (line) when they're not being "restimulated" by the outer environment.

So, the upper-level application of this and what it evolved into after delivering the material for "*The Tablets of Destiny*," is what we call "Analytical Recall." Where formerly we were talking about "resurfacing and reducing" emotional encoding and the imprinting on that, in "*Crystal Clear*" we emphasize the idea of "Analytical Recall," which could basically be anything...

The purpose behind this is that we actually found that sending an individual, that had very little experience or practice already with handling "mental imagery" or "memory" or any "recall" in *resurfacing* stuff that had emotional encoding on it—it wasn't as effective unless they were *first* introduced, and not to a point of being emotional charged or restimulated, but being brought through the basic elements of increasing abilities *of* "recall"—basically being able to pull up the imagery and the scenery; and we were talking about facets—the various (aspects) that are attached to the energy and the way that it is imprinted or encoded; *or* even "programmed," when it comes to "associative thought."

It's kind of interesting, because as much as we're "trained" or "conditioned" to do this—or to *not* do this—by our environment, by basically taking things for granted, or what we're told or using authority; this starts to bring an individual into learning more about their abilities as *Self*.

So, in Systemology we talk about examining the *facets*, which are any of the—we could talk about the "light-wave facets," the scenes, the places, the brightness, the symbols, the actual things or objects; the "sound-wave facets," language, speech, the loudness, the tone, you know, any background noise. When we talk about our encounters with objects or the encounters with sensory stimulus of "matter and particles," there's touch, feel, hardness, softness, smells, tastes.

And then, keep in mind, we *are* recording a "mental image"—we're recording the scenes, we're recording the actual events in our memory, you know, and giving all these other significances—so, we're talking about the motions and the actions; we're talking about anything that's taking place around us that's *other-determined*, even the sense that there's like a "wind" or the exterior or external temperature, or of the room, and so forth.

These are all *facets* of memory. An individual with low levels of beta-Awareness isn't using to the fact that so much of this actually being maintained or being carried with them when they're going about their everyday life. And an individual will always *think* they're applying *full* attention and full awareness to their management of life, because the *Self* —from the point-of-view of the Alpha-Spirit—it doesn't know any better unless it's actually allowed to know better in its beta-experience.

So, if those channels are "blocked"—or, you know, we talked about an emotional imprinting or turmoil and traumas and enforced realities and erroneous beliefs and all this; this becomes a totality of Awareness. It's still a totality, because it's the—essentially, the *limit* of what is capable at any given time; but it's not *all* of what is, you know, capable *in* totality.

Therefore, we use the Standard Model, we use the ZU-line, we use these gradient scales in which to kind of *gauge* where an individual is at; and an individual will, you know, tend to go through—we talked about the "Beta Awareness Scale" and so forth—we can go *through* (that) whole range of emotions and thoughts as we *run through* any of these experiences, or as we go through untangling that emotional—the energy that's kind of "wound up" to create those emotional *masses* and those *imprints.*

An individual may be just "fine" until something is brought into restimulation, and then as they run through it—for example, first they may feel completely hopeless about it and the essence of being, for example, "victimized" or so forth; and then they begin to feel the "loss" and "grief" associated with anything that's connected to the experience—I mean, even if it's the "loss" of skin cells with a scrape; I mean, any kind of "pain" or other-determined situation that causes a sensation in which the individual doesn't have command over, it can kind of restimulate different things.

"Small" things can later become very "big" things. An individual that's in a low state of Awareness—that's already accumulated large amounts of imprinting and is kind of going around as, you know, a "push-pull mechanism" on a reactive level—very small things *can* seem "catastrophic" within their reality.

Because, for example, stubbing your toe, or just some very simple mishaps of life, suddenly seem detrimental to survival and existence, because they're being dealt with—or viewed or experienced—*through* all these other "mental images" and imprints and so forth that have already put the person at the state of low awareness; a reactive mechanistic state.

For as much as we throw around the idea of the "upper-level" work—the upper Grades, or the "Wizard Grades"—the entire premise behind it, and the aspects that we're actually developing are really all set forth in Grade-III, and particularly "*Crystal Clear.*" The ideas behind handling the various emotional encoding, mental programming, the ability to work with "Analytical Recall," all of the basic elements of "beta-defragmentation," all the way up to some pretty *curious* and *esoteric* work is all relayed there. And these are the fundamentals on which any of the other work is dealt with. So, even at Grade-IV or with Piloting, we're still actually using "*Crystal Clear*" when we're working with individuals—and even working with our own "*defragmentation.*"

So, the idea of, kind of, working one step *beyond*, is one of the ways in which we've been able to make certain of the "Mastery" along the way—so, that the individuals that are actually presenting anything, particularly in the name of the Mardukite movement, are following to a particular standard; are adhering to a specific criteria, and that the graded level and the materials and the understanding that is accessible with these materials is duplicated across the board—that this is something that can be dispensed and disseminated from the Mardukite Academy and the Systemology Society; and then, having other "Master-level" participants, practitioners and instructors—at your own local levels—to be able to actually duplicate the same level of understanding as what can be achieved in working, for example, directly with *me* or *here* at the Mardukite Academy.

The basic principles, for example, have to do with: getting an individual to the point of *cause* as opposed to *effect*—and raising *beta-Awareness* in relationship to *Self-determination*. Even the things that you take for granted every day—the environment that you see around you, or the type of memory, or the type of information that's associated with that memory or other emotions or particular data and facts that have been attached to it—these are actually... These are all kind of running on "automatic" unless an individual is actually in a point of Self-determination—actually able to maintain some kind of command and control over these elements.

So, we do various practices in, for example, some of the first applications of "self-processing," we use what we call "Processing Command Lines"—we use the *command line* to, for example: "Recall a sound that was very loud." And then, in the beginning, we're kind of *prompting* the considerations of various facets—and these could be applied to almost anything; there's just some examples in there, such as: "Where was it?" "What was loud?" "What else did you see?"—you know, things of that nature. Basically, *recalling* something—and then really getting a *vivid*... Well, like I say, we call it "Recall"—it's a little bit...

Technically, we can say, "*remember*" also—we *could* use a term like "remember"; like, "Remember something..." But, "*recall*" seems to have more of a definitive element to it, to where we're actually bringing something *up*. In Route-1, we kind of use the idea of "*resurfacing*"; and then in Route-2, here in "*Crystal Clear*," we use the term "*recall*" and that's kind of the basis which this material was founded.

This is kind of a prerequisite to doing any further work with the Mind—to be able to actually manage the contents of which it is already working with. So, in that respect, that was: "Recall a sound that was very loud." You can also supplement that with: "Recall a sound that was very soothing," and kind of apply the same things, getting an individual...

I mean, this *seems* incredibly basic, but the upper-level of understanding—the kind of logic that goes behind this—the individual is actually able to *analyze*—which is why we call it "Analytical Recall"—they're actually able to *analyze* the *facets* that have been attached to this memory. So, the sensations, the ideas, the environment—anything that may be attached. And it may be, for example, in this kind of "lighter" Analytical Recall work, we're not dealing with something that's purely traumatic. I mean, if the first reactive memory that *hangs up* when you say, like, "Recall a sound that was very loud" and the first reaction is a violent memory... That's why we start to deal with the "tech" in "*The Tablets of Destiny*" before we even start handling something of this nature.

As simplistic as it seems, we are *aware* that it has the tendency—depending on the state of an individual or their control of the Mind–Body systems—to *trigger* reactive-response... well, *reactions* and *responses*; as opposed to choosing to recall something on a Self-determined level. For example, I can choose to recall a sound, for example, by *scanning* through times when this happened and *selecting* one—selectively taking one.

When we're dealing with "reactive memory," we want to make sure that we're *flattening*—and by that meaning: reducing any of the emotional or reactive-response mechanisms to that, if it's, for example, a scene that carries an emotional reaction. If an individual, you know, you say, "Recall a sound that's very loud," and something comes to mind, you know, a "bell ringing" when you were in school or so forth; that in and of itself may not be something very traumatic.

It's just analyzing—being able to pull up and analyze the facets attached to that.

Now, if you say "Recall a sound that was very loud" and the individual brings up the "collision" of a "car crash" or something violent—or an emotional charge to it—then, you know that this isn't something being treated at an *analytical* level. When they think of something "very loud," they're still, essentially, at a point, fixed, experiencing this point of "emotional trauma" or so forth—which may carry other physical sensations and other aspects. This is that "restimulative" aspect of the Human Condition that is not very well understood in, for example, the conventional sciences and medical fields and so forth; because, the idea that, for example, an individual is still carrying heavy charges of, for example, a "car crash"—and they are watching a film or something and there is something that is very similar to the situation...

Of course a person in a high point of "beta-Awareness," it's not... they're gonna see it and maybe there's some *tinges* of uncomfortability—maybe they're not fully actualized in that respect—but when an individual is at a *lower* level of beta-Awareness, different restimulative—you know, stimulation from the environment, such as seeing these scenes again, can actually *cause them* to experience a lot of the same facets and a lot of the same components to the original memory; because, it is being triggered from a low-level Awareness, when they're not really in command of thought and command as Self—and then, basically, responding with further other-determined "mental imagery" or "emotional encoding" that's basically setting up their experience.

And so, for, you know—it could be something as simple as a "headache" or it could be something, you know... Because of the way in which emotion is encoded, for example, an individual might have had this happen to them, and then they're at a friend's house and it's restimulated by watching a movie at the friend's house; there may be *later* association attributed to the "friend's house"—that location—or even that "friend," which are really passed on from the original encounter, the original *Imprinting Incident*, where the individual attached the idea that "a loud noise meant they were in danger" or there was a threat to them and so forth.

We see this also, for example, with "tone of voice" and so forth—an individual that, when they were younger and they had a lot of emotional imprinting experiences with someone with a certain kind of commanding "tone" or a certain type of "voice" or certain "stance" while they were doing it and so forth, we actually see those individuals at later points in life—depending on their level of Awareness; depending on how actualized they are—having an inability to *confront* or *face up* to those similar situations; so, you see people, you know, "shutting down" and even determining *likeness* and *dislike* solely based on these former experiences.

And it just may be some kind of happenstance situation—it may be that the person is actually not in danger and this is something that's just taking place; or they're even passively observing it taking place with others. Again, this is one of those elements, when we talk about "circuits" and all the various ways on a ZU-line—or as someone carries their "Personal Identity Continuum" with them—that there's all these different associations, not *just* on what's happened to them, but what they've done to others, and also them, what they've experienced *others* doing to others; all of this being considered elements of what an individual holds as their experience.

This information may be very *erroneous*; it may be that certain associations of what's considered *helpful* or *harmful*, actually have nothing to do with the actuality of the way things are; *but*, due to emotional imprinting and due to the way in which all this is encoded, the way in which even "learned knowledge" to associate it as data can be "programmed"—well, there you have it; this is the basic state from where we are operating from as an Awareness.

And so, "*Crystal Clear*" includes *many* of these various—at an introductory level, when we're just dealing with Awareness—it includes all of these various ways and examples of which this could be applied; and it's not limited to *just* what's in this book; and that's something, too, why again, when we're talking about someone who is applying assistance as a Minister, or an individual that's being professionally trained to be a "Pilot" to actually *administer* even upper-level techniques—it really has to do with their own level of Mastery, which is why the Master Course is important no matter where an individual goes *from* there. But, it has to do with their own Mastery and their own (intuition) *beyond that*; beyond what is just learned in books. The certainty can only be achieved through its application.

As an individual is able to *apply*, for example, the philosophies of Systemology and able to actually look through the Master Course—or even at the lower Grades—validating for themselves, the things that we have put forth or expressed, *are* actually as they *are*. This raises that level of certainty and the ability to *reach*, the *willingness* to do things, and then, actually yield the effects, by going out and actually practicing this and seeing it, you know, for yourself.

None of this is, you know, *faith-based*; none of this is, in regards to looking for something *else* or trying to focus on a lifetime *after* this one—when we're dealing with Grade-III, we're dealing very much with *this* lifetime as things are presently experienced in beta-existence.

A lot of the other elements that I've thrown in with this Master Course, even beyond the Mardukite Master-level—other things that I've been expressing—to try to slowly raise everyone's level of Awareness even *beyond* what is just relayed in Grade-III. But, this is what we're doing now—and I believe that with the proper study, the proper application, of these techniques that you can go forth and practice these things and see the effective results for yourself.

: LECTURE 47—ACTUALIZATION TECH :
(September 30, 2020)

[Okay, here we are now—what are we at? We're at lecture forty-seven; so, I guess given how little time we have left, I suppose we should actually get serious about learning some stuff. No, seriously though—the amount of time that it would actually take to really delve into every facet of Mardukite Systemology, really it's deserving of its own course. It's for that reason that, as I say...]

My main concern is making certain that a Master-level of understanding is attainable by an individual that's looking to achieve the ends that are set out through all three Grades. To also basically make certain that even if you don't come away from the Course period—the lecture period of these courses—knowing every single facet of all the work that has been put forth in the last *twenty-five* years, the idea being that you're familiar enough with the materials that it doesn't seem like this ominous stack of paper—or these textbooks, which are essentially "bricks" of knowledge that can sit on a shelf for long periods of time, with individuals feeling too intimidated to delve into them.

Part of the idea behind the Mardukite Master Course is to familiarize an individual enough to be able to delve into the material directly; because for the amount of lectures that we've spent covering the entire scope of the Mardukite Master Course, we could apply this same amount of attention, energy and time, directed specifically at Mardukite Systemology and the development of Systemology and all of the facets in which you could implement it.

What I've really been doing is going through the *highlights*—we've talked about, essentially, *today*, the fundamentals behind *"Crystal Clear"* and the epitome of the Grade-III work; where it culminated to. And we've been talking about the elementary application of the *tech*, in terms of elevating or increasing Awareness—which, of course, naturally leads us toward points of greater Self-Actualization; which runs pretty much parallel with "beta-defragmentation"—the amount of beta-Awareness as *Actualized Awareness* that an individual is carrying with them in their everyday life.

Even in the scope of the work—only the principles and fundamentals meant to get someone *going* in the right direction, were even established, even with all the material that went into Grade-III. And the idea is not whether or not *I have* been able to make this work for myself—if *I've been able* to make it effective—the point was whether or not it could be duplicated and relayed in a manner, such as instruction, and in books that could be administered *without* the assistance of a "Pilot" or without *my* particular direct attention—for example, as an apprenticeship or mentorship—that this could be carried forth.

I stand behind the work—especially through Grade-III—as far as its development and what validation an individual would find if they were to practice any of this, or even go and looking for the historical research to support the previous Grades and so forth—this is all pretty sound; and we've been using it as a stepping point to get to higher-levels.

Because, you know, it sounds really "esoteric" when I mention things about *higher* Grades—for example, the idea about the "*circuits*" is actually found right within the work of Self-Actualization in "*Crystal Clear.*" [*Let me see, we got some... just looking at some of these Command Lines here...*] Oh, for example: "Recall an incident when you were invalidated by someone." "Recall an incident when you invalidated someone else." "Recall an incident when someone invalidated someone else."

Although the wording and sequencing of this might not be as perfected as we might apply it from a Grade-IV perspective—after putting "Piloted Processing" in a practice further

—there you have the *three circuits*. Like I said, these are a little bit out of order in how we treat them at higher levels. For example, *Circuit-1*: we would have an individual *doing* something; so, for example, an "incident where *they* invalidated someone else"—and then thinking out the *facets* regarding that. And *then* an incident when someone else invalidated them.

And this sequence—when we consider the idea of, you know, "doing unto others" and the idea that an individual carries around experiences with them that the only reason we would ever want to hold onto something or keep something is with the intention that we were going to *use* it in some way. So, a lot of times you see individuals at low-levels of Awareness actually acting out—or (dramatizing)—the exact things that have taken place to them; or in this example, also *Circuit-3*, which would be things that are happening—things that are being "witnessed"; so, whether or not it's happening *to you*, or you're *doing it*, now you're *seeing it* taking place "out there"—you're still registering that information, that data, in connection to what you consider your experience and in connection to how you're going to treat certain circumstances at a later point.

And so the idea isn't that we're going to "brainwash" an individual or we're going to "remove their memory" or given them some sort of "amnesia"—the idea being that all the information and memory that someone is carrying around with them, that they don't necessarily feel the compulsion to *have* to use it; that just because they've seen something take place, or something has happened to them, and so on and so forth, that the automatic mechanism that kicks in that basically causes these tendencies to repeat, that they don't have to participate in that.

That's when we start to see an increase in Self-determination—that Awareness—that *actual* participation *by* Self in the activity and the moment-to-moment experience of everyday life and the Human Condition. Because otherwise, this is all running on "automatic" and those that have perfected an understanding of this knowledge, for even decades now—because I've basically been piecing together the stuff that has come through in the types of... like, when you look at "Creative Psychology," and you know I mentioned Carl Jung and Timothy Leary; when you look at the conspiratorial aspects of the past hundred years concerning the study of the Mind—the study of the Human Condition, rather—and its behavioral characteristics, "mind control" and so forth.

All of this has brought us to where we are in terms of our knowledge base and what we can *reference* and what we can *research* concerning this whole thing that we consider as the Human Condition.

Now, when we consider the "abilities" of the individual—the *creative ability*; when we consider an individual's *willingness* to *do*, *willingness* to *reach*—and what their actual ability is—we connect that to their actual state or condition. An individual that is more *actualized*, has more *ability*—simple as that. An individual that has more command and control over the Mind, is going to be able to *use* those systems or functions to basically *engage in a better Game*—engage in a better experience of the Human Condition *in* beta-existence.

So, when we start reaching into further examples of "systematic processing"—we've already talked about "*resurfacing*" to reduce emotional connectivity, or the emotional charge on things; we've talked about "*recalling*" to *analyze* the various facets involved, to be able to basically untangle this whole mess or "web" or interconnected data and knowledge and programming and encoding that's taken place; and then of course, by doing this, we can actually apply the higher faculties of the Mind.

One example being: "thought experiments"—this was something that was discussed by Albert Einstein, when asked or when discussing the ability to perceive the point-of-view of, for example, a photon of light, to be able to actually perceive what different things would be taking place at a level of which weren't able to observe at the time with a microscope and so forth; his theories were developed as a result of "thought experiments"—the ability to actually use the Mind to imagine things *accurately*; not just imagining scenery and beautiful pictures, but being able to use the knowledge of physical systems or the knowledge of considerations—at whatever level you're dealing with—and actually be able to experience the point-of-view of something that is not otherwise already taking place.

Now, when we consider what we mean when we imply that —we're talking about "imagining"; we're talking about "thought"; we're talking about "mental imagery" —this is what a lot of individuals would consider *play*—and the reason being is because they've stopped doing this; when we think about what a child is doing when they're *pretending*, they're giving a "pretense" to what is actually taking place; they are acting as though *this is* happening *now*—something they could formulate for future use is being *practiced*.

We tend to—the funny thing is, we tend to disregard such things as: "Oh, well, that's just imaginative child stuff"— well funny enough, this "imaginative child stuff" seems to be a little more powerful than what many people give it credit for, when we talk about the considerations and beliefs of society.

When we consider about someone—the Actualized Awareness of an individual—we consider that their ability to direct and project Self, and project the *Will* of *Self* and reach into the *future* is basically distinguished by the higher heightened states of Awareness.

So, you have individuals that are, for example, still stuck in some kind of *past* experience that tend to come in lower on the "Beta-Awareness Test." When you are applying some kind of quantification or evaluation to these states, you find that those, for example, scoring "1.4" or *lower* had recently experienced significant lost, or they had not successfully recovered awareness in their personal stores of ZU from a previous—even if it's potentially a distant point in terms of time or duration.

For their purposes, it's actually still happening—it's still in restimulation in present time; the individual is still going about life as though they are still reacting or responding towards this event as if it's still taking place. I mean, that's pretty significant. And to be honest, when we talk about old-school definitions or even NexGen definitions of what it would mean to be "psychotic."

A "psychotic" in this respect, would be someone who is literally *stuck* in the past, that's basically still living out this experience—which is why, I mean, when you've seen. I've spent time with these types of individuals; not only in an academic setting while studying psychology, but I've lived with them without any kind of protective bars so to speak, particularly when I spent time in California. I've seen many of these individuals—once they basically shut down the asylums, because the asylums aren't any good; you know, so many horror stories about the type of practices that were going on—we won't even get into that.

But the final result of this was that, rather than funding mental health institutions, the individuals that would otherwise be institutionalized or at least be able to have a controlled environment to work from—of course, our Systemology is not really aimed toward that application—but, that type of funding ended up being signed over to the individual themselves on the idea that well, they'll be given a certain monthly allotment and the idea was that they would be able to manage themselves; and of course, most have an inability to do that, in spite of even the best case-workers.

So, you have a lot of individuals on the West Coast running the streets that are actually, for all intents and purposes, either psychotic or neurotic—and we'll get into the difference here in a second; but, we're dealing with those that... you've seen them interact or perhaps they are shouting at a wall, right? Well, they're *not* shouting at a wall. That's not —they don't even really *perceive* the wall. They're locked into this experience. And it can be quite scary for an individual—you know, someone else on the *outside*—to be a participant or be a witness to some of these behaviors going on. But, once one actually understands, it's a little different.

Then, those scoring between "1.5" and "2.2" on the "Beta Awareness Test" or "Beta Awareness Scale" generally experienced significant *invalidation* or *enforcement* of reality— and had not really recovered from this. And we're talking about authority; we're talking about the invalidation of Self; the invalidation of knowledge—an individual that is constantly "*stopped*" in their activities: this creates a "neurotic."

This creates someone that is essentially still trying to break free of a reactive point. They are not so far down, necessarily, that they are continually repeating the trauma over and over again, but they're becoming incredibly *complacent* and still be operated as a "push–pull mechanism" because their *Will* to *do* and *reach* has been thwarted so many times that they've just stopped.

And this is a little different than an individual a little bit higher up—for example, when you start to get into the level between "2" and "3"—you're dealing with someone that's just kind of circling loops or hitting against *barriers* in various—we talked about the "Figure-8." Their ability to maintain a *high* level of beta-Awareness is usually being blocked by some kind of emotional consideration.

Because there's *still* all these little personal triggers [within the range of "2" and "3"] to where an individual can be doing fine—going along in life—and then some little thing comes up, that to other individuals actually seems rather arbitrary or minimal, but it ends up being this, you know, "devastating life-threatening situation" to *that* individual.

And so, the idea of Beta-Awareness levels and the idea of these "shifting states" between *emotions* and *thought* is not, you know—being "actualized" and going to the point of "beta-defragmentation"—the idea is not that you will somehow apply this topmost state of "enthusiasm" to everything at all times in all waking hours of the day; I mean, of course that's what we're striving for—we're striving to have this point—but the practices that we're treating in Mardukite Systemology simply move toward that direction, almost as an absolute. It's not meant to guarantee that one is going to achieve it; it's showing that this *mode* of operation—this *Pathways*—does deliver one to higher and higher points.

You know, we've got individuals that have been still receiving benefit—that have been working with *"Crystal Clear"* every single day for a *year*. And they are *still* receiving (gains) from it. So, the idea that as a finite book—or treating Grade-III as a finite level—that there's a finite point, necessarily, reached in and of itself... Well, I... I guess that depends on what your opinion of "Mastery" is—because, in some respects, the route of "Mastery" could continue on for the course of one's lifetime; every step of the way, each being one more point of "Mastery."

But at this point, when we're starting to deal with stuff of this caliber, we are approaching a level of wisdom—a level of knowledge, a level of practical application, in terms of communication, attention, awareness—we are approaching those points that have been alluded to: this "Wizard Level"—this idea of the "actualized individual" that has already gone through the type of the work that we've been dealing with in the Mardukite Master Course and can actually demonstrate that they have this *quality* to them; that they're kind of a step *above* the "average." So, that's what we consider, when we're starting to move on beyond the "Master levels" into the "Wizard Grades."

Okay, another one of the points here—because I want to make sure we get through as much of this "Actualization Tech" as possible; as I say, we could have dedicated an entire course to *this*. So, when we talk about establishing these points along the *Pathway to Self-Honesty*, and what we've done is establish a "map" with Grade-III. The map is not the journey; it isn't the end-all of everything—it isn't the final word on what we can develop with this—it's simply a point of *realization*.

And as I've stated in the text: "*realization precedes actualization.*" An individual has to be able to *realize* something *before* it can be *actualized* for them. So, realizing something is possible; realizing that something can be known; realizing that help is available; realizing that an individual *can* achieve greater states of Self-determinism—these are all necessary *before* you can [*laughs*] actually *actualize* these states.

It seems like a lot of "psychology" or "mysticism" or "metaphysics" up until the point in, you know, the "Master Grades" when we're actually going: "Oh, I see. This is actually possible. Oh! This is actually the way things are. Oh!" Prior, a lot of this is treated as a *huge* "Mystery."

And some people to this day, no matter how much you show to them, they're still stuck on a fact that this stuff can't be known—and that the Human Condition or the Mind and all these things *must* be too complicated or too far out of our reach to have any reality on it.

Well... I think we've established now that that's *bull.*

But, more to the point is: what can we do with this? And that's basically what Mardukite Systemology was to represent is: what can we do with this? I had been studying—other individual had been—all this ancient wisdom and these concepts and these rituals and, you know, trying to elevate our state of Being and actualized point-of-view...

Well, you know, obviously, we still had room to grow; and that is what allowed us to examine all this type of stuff at Grade-I and Grade-II and still contrast, demonstrate, represent and develop "Mardukite Systemology" as something (quote; unquote) "separate" from that; that this is not a rehash of doing the same things that have already been done in the last 6,000 years—we're breaking new ground now.

And so—just as "realization precedes actualization," well before you can actualize the potential of the Spirit as Self, you have to realize that you *are* the Spirit as Self; and although some people can, you know, "Well, yeah, of course, I know I'm not my body and la-dee-dah." We talked about that already: that an individual doesn't *have* a Spirit; an individual *is* Spirit.

Unless this point of knowingness and certainty can be established, a lot of this is going to seem like it still requires faith—like it still may not, you know, be something solid—because an individual is still operating from the point-of-view of the genetic vehicle, not the point-of-view of Self. And if nothing else, *that* is what we are looking to resolve when we work through, for example, "*Crystal Clear*" in Grade-III Mardukite Systemology.

So, in essence, our actions—our efforts—are only limited to the extent that we can imagine, that we can take "right knowledge" and apply a proper evaluation of "personal effort" in light of "right experience" or "Cosmic Law" of cause and effect and in accordance with Will. And what is that?—We're going right back to our original concept of "magic" right? The ability to command in accordance with *Will.*

And what we're taught is that in beta-existence, in the Physical Universe, *action follows thought*—the Mind-System engages the command and control of the body and directs something; but an Alpha-existence, *thought follows action*—thought is essentially the direction of energy-flow and creative ability *of* the Alpha-Spirit.

So, we see this kind of moving the down the spectrum at various intervals between various relay stations. For example, if you consider the circuits of communication—any two points along the ZU-line can be points of communication; they can be relays to one another. So, they're trading off being the "sender" or "receiver"; or the "cause-point" and the "effect-point" so to speak.

And so, the idea then of "imagination"—we brought up "thought experiments"—this is kind of a *key* into delivering an individual into greater considerations of Self and to higher points of actualization; it seems like "child's play" at times, but maybe there is something to be learned there, however.

In pointing all of this out, we have, as I say, the *seeds* of everything we're treating in Grade-IV Systemology is *potentially* established right here in Grade-III. And so, even when we talk about the "Standard Operating Procedure" that we apply for Piloting at Grade-IV—the elements of those, the routes of those, are pretty much established in Grade-III, as far as their points of fact and their effectiveness.

Now, we've been fine-tuning this as we go along—along the upper paths—but, you know, so we talked about Route-1 as given in *"The Tablets of Destiny"*; we talked about Route-2 —"Analytical Recall." Route-3, as it's treated in the Standard Operating Procedures of Grade-IV Systemology is actually the "Three Circuits" as we were describing them: doing things to others; others doing to Self; witnessing others doing things to others—these are the "Three Circuits" that are treated in Route-3, which is basically a more refined version of what we've been talking about.

And then this idea of "imagining"—the ability to freely "imagine"—and work freely, you know, *fluidly*, with the Mind-System; thought-experiments, creations, all kinds of abilities of the Self—this is what we treat as A.T. or Route-0, or essentially the upper-most point of *processing*. Because, once we're done working through all this reactive work and various mental programming, we're basically playing with "what can Self do?" in this new *cleared sphere* of existence—this kind of Personal Universe—to be able to create and destroy various mental images; to be able to conceive of all kinds of things; whether or not they have any place or coexistence with the Physical Universe is irrelevant.

The idea is to get an individual *free* of only considering and thinking in terms of *agreements* with the Physical Universe.

I don't mean to glorify—the reason I bring up examples from Einstein and thought-experiments is because of how much emphasis is put on him as being an innovative inventor and creative mind and putting forth ideas and concepts at a time when we're only now, a hundred years or so after the fact, able to validate and actually apply various things.

Don't forget though: the equations of Einstein were also used to develop the *atomic bomb*; so I'm not trying to glorify this individual. But, what I'm saying is, when you have, for example, in this quote here: "Imagination is more important than knowledge; for knowledge is limited to all we know and understand, while imagination embraces the entire world and all there ever will be to know and understand."

When you have the individual who has treated, as an academic level—as a scientific level—put so high on the pedestal; and this individual is basically sitting there telling you, "Well, why don't you focus on imagination. Because that's really the key to all this; and that's how I've gotten to where I'm going."

Now, we can sit there and only have all these high I.Q. People being able to later understand and treat the equations—and being able to duplicate applications of all these "high scientific" ideas—but *conceptually*, the very fact they would have to be *realized* before they could be *actualized*, came down to the point of using "thought experiments"—

using the ability of imagination in an actual control of the Mind-System *outside* the parameters of what's "given."

These aren't individuals who are taking what's already "given" and just making it better; these are individuals that, you know—we use this term "outside the box." Well, there is no "outside the box" anymore, because everyone's used that term *too much*. They just end up in another box—but, we're talking about individuals who are able to *supersede*—go *beyond*—what has been "given"; what has been established.

And this is what we talk about when we move into "*Metahuman Destinations*"—I mean, this is what the *Pathway to Self-Honesty* and upward is all about; It's all about using the functions of the Human experience *beyond* this mediocre mundane dry enforced reality, you know, way of going about things. Those considerations are only going to lead us to lower and lower points of existence as we go on.

This isn't the only Universe that's ever existed; and it's not the only Universe we have occupied—nor is it the lowest point of existence that we could potentially occupy our Beingness as a point-of-view.

And if we keep going in the direction—as a society, as a Human Condition—that it's going in: that's pretty much where we are going to end up in. So, part of this "Cosmic Rescue Mission"—without getting too esoteric—I'm here trying to get a certain baseline across of a solid ledge—and here we're treating it as the Mardukite Master Course—a solid ledge; nothing that goes to extreme; nothing that seems to far reaching, in being able to establish a standpoint by which we can actually develop further.

Behind the scenes now, between the Academy and the Systemology Society and the development of Mardukite Zuism —yeah, of course, we *are* working further; but the point again, is being able to duplicate these efforts on a broad scale—and to be able to do it outside of just my own efforts;

to be able to bring an individual up to the level of certainty, the level of knowledge, the level of Awareness, for example, that I just have simply been demonstrating for the last decade in delivering and elevating the Mardukite movement.

When we say: *"thoughts are things"*—well, that's because an individual puts so much *substance* into them, thought-formed beliefs and so forth. Thoughts don't really need to be *things*—thoughts can be fluidly handled without any kind of emotional attachment, without any kind of solidity being given to them. The ability to direct thought is not contingent on it being a solid object.

Really, the idea here being: that the individual has a fluid range of thought; should be able to conceive of anything. This is something we deal with more specifically at Grade-IV, but the handling of "mental imagery"—the control of *thought*—is really important at *any* level; it's not just specific to only certain Grades.

There's this concept of "Alpha Thought" versus "Beta-Thought." You have your "beta-thought," which is connected to the *interior* of the "Mind-System" when its related to the Human Condition in beta-existence; and "Alpha-thought" being simply the thought of *Self*—*Self* directing thought in the form, for example, of a "postulate" or the application of *Will*.

This is applying or being directed from Alpha-thought, which is different—it's basically the clear, like what we're talking about with Imagination, it's just a clear production of anything. I mean, in the Spiritual Universe, back in, you know, where the Alpha-Spirit resides and actually exists as a point-of-view or point-of-Awareness that's emanating, well, anything can be willed into being, anything can be constructed, anything can be considered.

It's only within *this* material existence that we've started to treat *thought* as an "effort"—treating it with the idea that: to do anything mentally requires the same kind of effort as to carry it out physically. That's one of those *fragmentations* of the physical conditions; that's not an actual truth. The truth is that an individual can be operating with *thought* indefinitely and literally expending no physical energy in the process of it.

Most of the fatigue and lower states of Awareness and so forth, come in due to states of *fragmentation*; that's not due to the *actual* creative ability of the Self. The Self isn't the one getting "tired." It's *other* things being stimulated that are just kind of like impressing or increasing the "pressure," like the pressure in an environment or weather, so to speak; more and more of the considerations and imprints and masses and thoughtformed beliefs are being *impressed* upon the individual—impinging upon *them*, instead of *their* will impinging upon the environment, an automatically created-projected environment, which *Self* is participating in—it's using the energy of *Self* to do it—but the reason it's generating fatigue and the reason there's fragmentation is because the individual is kind of pulled into it unknowingly.

They don't *know* they're creating or putting all this energy into this experience, because (to them) it's all happening automatically, so it becomes—as they become more and more the effect of it; as they lose this kind of certainty or reach or command and control to direct it—that's where a lot of the diminishing qualities of the Human Condition begin to take effect.

And we see this not only with an individual as they deal with, for example, energy flows, attention and awareness during the day, but we see it accumulate over the course of one's lifetime. And a reflection of that: we can assume that the Spirit has been doing the same thing with each incarnation—we conceive that there's this diminished ability to consider anything *higher* than what's come before.

So, it's kind of like compounding onto itself—and so, the same way that we carry more and more with us over the course of this lifetime; we're carrying more and more with us over the course of several lifetimes. And of course, we're not getting too much into "past-lives" and all of that at Grade-III, but most individuals that are treating this—most individuals that are involved in the "New Age"—most individuals that are dealing with various alternative spiritualities and anything that might be culminated as entry-points to get them onto this pathway, they kind of already have an inkling of that; they already have some kind of intuitive consideration that they understand the "Immortality of the Spirit," they understand that they have "lived before"—some even believing they have certain "recall" accessible from that.

For whatever it is—we know that there is another aspect to this, but for *our* intents and purposes, the "beta-defragmentation"—the level of Awareness we're trying to get an individual, or you getting your Seekers to that you're working with, or even yourself—this is what qualifies a "Master-level" or a "Master Grade" aspect.

Like, I can sit here and go through the materials with you and instruct you in the various practices and what they say in the books and so forth—but, of course, I am also delivering to *you* as an individual; not just you going out and being an instructor and representing our path—but, yeah, of course, we wanted to make sure we were doing that on a certain structured level where we are all on the same page.

But, more to the point—the idea of what we're culminating with, for example, Grade-III Mardukite Systemology and the work in *"The Tablets of Destiny"* and *"Crystal Clear"* and everything that composes *"The Systemology Handbook"* as a Grade-III textbook—this is what we're considering a Master-level of realization and actualization in relation to the Human Condition.

So, if *you* can achieve these points; if *you* can work through this material; if *you* can work through these books; and *you* can understand the intellectual part of it and its delivery, to be able to talk as I have, to another individual and work them through it as well—*then* you have achieved the Master-level.

: LECTURE 48—GRADUATION, FINAL LECTURE :
(September 30, 2020)

[*Okay, we're running a little over on time now—we're talking about Awareness Tech, Self-Actualization, the application of "Crystal Clear"—and that's okay; I mean, we're now at the last lecture of the Mardukite Master Course—we're at the point where I'm trying to deliver you to this certainty that we've been able to cover, and the materials, throughout the course of... I mean, this is now four textbooks...*]

We got 3,600 pages of information here—we "*The Great Magickal Arcanum,*" "*Merlyn's Complete Book of Druidism,*" "*Necronomicon: The Complete Anunnaki Legacy*" and now "*The Systemology Handbook.*" We're culminating, essentially, *twenty-five* years of research and discovery that's led to the current and future work regarding the Church of Mardukite Zuism *and* The Systemology Society.

We're basically capping off this material as what is considered the Master Grade—Grade-III—for Mardukite Systemology, the Master-level of understanding and application of it; being able to "*certify*" you as an "Instructor" that are able to deliver this information and basically demonstrate that if you have the certainty and you've done the work and you've been able to duplicate our level of understanding from the (Academy) in your own personal environment—well, then, being "empowered" to, as I say, carry the "Mardukite" work forward in everyday life.

And not just your own personal explorations and personal development, but again—we're looking to the establishment, in the future here, of more "study groups," more divisions of the "Academy," other branches and "lodges" of The Systemology Society and even the Church of Mardukite Zuism.

So, we're establishing, basically, the point here where we can kind of send everyone in their own directions, depending on what that is; because, we've been able to establish a cohesive common ground understanding of all the work that has led up to this point.

I mean, I could easily go on for several more days, just with the work involved with the *"Crystal Clear"* volume alone—and *still* not reach everything that's involved with that. But, of course, here—we *do still* have some time left, I want to make sure since we already have you here, I want to go over some more of the points that are put across in (*"Crystal Clear"*) so that we can feel like we have an even better coverage of the subject before sending you off on your own.

The work in our Systemology is actually relatively—particularly *"Crystal Clear"*—it's relatively safe to experiment with and develop on your own. So, the idea here that we are covering at the Mardukite Master Course level, the knowledge-base aspects of it—the intellectual—to establish the right comprehension and understanding beyond me just talking to you or assisting or, you know, what's given strictly in the books when you're reading on your own—so that you can actually participate in developing along the *Pathway* on your own, and actually *practice* these methods.

None of it is actually going to get you in any trouble, anything that's relayed in *"Crystal Clear"*—in fact, its meant to be as "non-restimulative" as possible, in just increasing an individual's attention, awareness, the ability to recall facets, increase in memory, various facets of the mind—the analytical abilities—and so forth.

We're trying to increase an individual's abilities at this point, before we throw them into anything more critical. Technically, when we were talking about the ability to handle "Human problems" in general, to confront conflict and things that we're protesting against—the idea of being able to actually *deal* with changes in our environment—and so forth; I deal a lot more with those particular aspects at Grade-IV, with the intent that there's probably going to be "Piloted" assistance with that.

Now, just like the way *"Crystal Clear"* is given, an individual can work their own way through Grade-IV without "Piloted" assistance as well. But the idea was that: we want to increase—before we start tackling... Well, one of the things we learned in treating *"resurfacing"* as it's given in *"The Tablets of Destiny"* as abbreactive therapies for emotional encoding, is that really the ability for an individual to handle that was dependent on their ability to just handle everyday life.

I mean, the ones that were more aware, the ones that were more actualized—the ones that had greater certainty—they had a *better* chance of directly confronting all this stuff without, you know, *falling into it*. Basically, when you're treating this on your own, one of the things that can happen —which is why we like the Piloted experience—is that an individual can kind of get stuck in a "loop" *and* there's nobody really there to assist them, so this process-program just kind of continues to get *run* and if it isn't—like we say, like *flattened*—sent back into its state of potential and is still being treated as these heavy *imprints* and emotional encoding —well, by themselves an individual *can* get "lost" in that.

And so, that's one of the things we don't really want to happen; because that's one of the ways—you know, when we're talking about pitfalls and traps and so forth in any of the materials during the course of this—well, in this instance, it would really be an individual that: *because* of the lack of Actualized Awareness and beta-defragmentation *already*, concerning the other skills they could have been working on, rather than just targeting all of these significant events directly from the start.

We found that it increased their ability—and then, of course, it led to what we consider *higher* states and more *ac-*

tualized applications that we now apply specifically at the Wizard levels; but all of that was developed from "*Crystal Clear*" and the application of Grade-III Mardukite Systemology.

I mean, just as we've progressed continuously from one "Route" to another—or one "Grade" to another—and then smoothly, for example, (transitioned) even from Mesopotamia *into* Mardukite Systemology, the same thing continues as we move upward. There's no—really, there's no *steep* drop-offs; there's no point in which the plateaus don't have another plateau that can't be baby-stepped up to.

That's not what we're doing here, because that's what a lot of other traditions have done: they've stuck an individual up on a *plateau* and they find themselves, basically, before this *chasm* of, you know, abyssal nothingness all around them; so they spend their entire existence working themselves up and rather than it leading to something greater, now they're sitting there basically on a rocky cliff, and they're going: "Well, what the hell do I do now? I don't know... Where does it go from here?"

Well, we don't have that in our *Pathway to Self-Honesty* and our *Gates to Infinity*; our pathway—the "map"—and of course, the map is not the journey; but the map, thus far, has been able to be laid out very very clearly, of which can—you know, not only as myself and other individuals that I've worked with directly, but now, my goal is that *others* outside of those that are just a part of—or have been working closely with—the Mardukite Academy, or even myself, directly over the past several years, have the ability to take what we have been doing—take what I've been doing for a quarter-of-a-century—but take what we have been doing, and establish, and be able to deliver effects.

I mean, not only experience them for yourselves—but actually be able to go out and deliver this to other people. And that's one of the things we kind of emphasize more in the

Wizard Grades; because, you know, we're working on all this ourselves, we've reached a point of at least enough stability to be able to encounter and deal with the *operations* of it with other individuals—and that's the kind of *spread* that we expect to happen to increase Awareness to create this better world.

I don't expect to reach, necessarily, every individual out on the planet directly by words—but, when so many people are out there that have heard them; so many individuals begin to apply and use this and then go out and be able to live their lives out in the world at large—the effects of this *are* going to spread; it's undoubtedly going to *spread*. But that requires, again, the efforts being faced, more than just myself.

Although we've had various staff members come and go; I've moved the offices I don't know how many times in the course of *thirteen* years—we're much more stable now. We first had a five-acre vacant land site that we were use for astronomical observation and energy experiments and so forth; but we weren't really able to develop and establish it very much as vacant land.

And so, about *eleven miles* southwest of that—we called that land "Mardukite Babylon"—and eleven miles southwest of there, just as in ancient times, eleven miles southwest of Babylon, you found "Borsippa," which was the—we talked about this for Mesopotamia—but basically where the Nabu scribe-priests and the development of the tradition in terms of the "tablet culture"—the cuneiform tablets and writing—and all that; that was all based there.

That's actually where we have established the new Headquarters. The new Headquarters here being in Monte Vista—and this is San Luis Valley—and we've been basically spending the last several years, in addition to doing the work, the last several years have been actually toward the development and solidification of a presence; a presence for not only the Church of Mardukite Zuism, but also the Systemology Society—a Headquarters so that this work can continue onward.

And then we are solidifying the actual state of the work now, with the Mardukite Master Course and the Master-Grade *volumes* and the Joshua Free Imprint publications which are allowing the material to reach well beyond what our distribution reach was before, when we were just "self-publishing."

So, we're working forward and we're moving forward; and this is dependent on individuals *like yourself*, that are attaining an Master-level understanding of the material, that are attaining personal *Self-Mastery* using the material—and a comprehension of it to such degree that they're able to actually go out into the world, or set up whatever aspects or elements or factions of our divisions—that they can actually administrate this stuff far beyond just the reach of our offices and Headquarters. Now, to basically get us a little farther through, I want to skim some of the points here of *"Crystal Clear"* that are particularly significant in its application. So...

Personal Fragmentation comes into effect primarily when: *a)* an individual is lost in the effects of their own thought-forms—which is an illusion—and is no longer actualizing awareness as cause; *b)* an individual is unable to freely change the effects of their Alpha-thought and continues to run on some former programming—which is now a fixed postulate or belief; *c)* an individual is inadequately analyzing environmental information and evaluating the efforts necessary to change or create an effect—and this is due to imprints and what is considered in previous schools, conditioning; *d)* an individual is unable to charge thoughts with effort to manifest or materialize their will—because emotional energy is wound up in imprint stores and reactive (mechanisms); and/or *e)* an individual is restrained from using, applying or expressing their individual Alpha-thought

—due to authoritarianism, educational programming, social pressure and other deterrents to Self-Honest beta-experience as a result of poorly managed experience.

So—there you have it; those are the key reasons for "personal fragmentation." I'm sure you can see many ways in which they can apply—apply to yourself; apply to people you know. And these are the key points that we are seeking to systematically correct in the Human Condition as we go forward with our Systemology.

In summary, we know that the Standard Model of Systemology is essentially showing that the Self—up at "7.0"—is carrying Alpha Thoughts—at "6.0"—as intention (at "5.0") from a Spiritual Beingness or "spiritual consciousness" or what we consider Alpha-experience, *to* a mental knowingness or a mental-consciousness, which is then carried into, and realized for, the Physical Universe by beta-thought —"4.0" or below—of a "beta-lifeform," which is connected on the ZU-line or the Identity—Personal Identity Continuum —*to* Self.

And so the Self is basically sending a directed current of energy down the ZU-line channel and it's interacting with all these points before it comes out the other end as an *effect*.

Now, when we talk about *Intention* or *Will*—an "intention" is basically always to "Self-direct" as *Cause* an *Effect* or to apply an "effort" to change some condition in existence, such as to "cause" a thing or condition to *be* or *not be*; to cause a cycle to *begin* or *end*; to cause a system to *start* or *stop*; or to cause a change in some variable. These would be elements of an application of "Alpha-thought" when being directed towards—well, whatever Sphere of Existence you're applying it to—but, that is basically the channel in which it's traveling. And that's what we're demonstrating with our Standard Model—and particularly, the ZU-line.

And when we talk about the *Ability* to direct personal *Awareness*—or to Self-direct Alpha-thought or Intention—or even working a "Command Line" for a *process*; we want an individual to consider, for example, the Seeker, to consider the questions of "Who is in control of your life?" You know? "Who are *you* accepting commands from?" "Who is directing your attention?" "Who is *requiring* that you direct your attention in such a way?" And "Who is demanding that you pay attention to them?" "Who is commanding that you listen to them?" You know?

Consider these elements when you're applying "beta-defragmentation"; because, you may find that an individual is actually taking on some of the characteristics of these "stronger" personalities in their life. Because they've learned that that's maybe one of the ways to "get on" or one of the ways to "survive."

Another thing an individual does is: they have the tendency to take on "weaker"—the qualities of *weaker* personalities that they've encountered in their life—because they've found that those individuals receive "assistance"—or rather "sympathy," which is *the lowest* level of energetic communication you could have with an individual.

Because what can you do? For example, you're a Mardukite Minister or a Systemology Pilot or a Master trying to make... That at the best: you could actually *do* something—you could *help* an individual, you know? Second best: you might be able to make an individual more *comfortable*—have them get along a little better in their physical existence as it is, or diminish their suffering a little; and this seems to be about the point that we get with Grade-II, for example.

So these three tiers—to actually *do* something, I think we've realized a little bit more clearly at Systemology at Grade-III. You know, the ability to *get by* a little bit better in the world is something, I think we've established by the time a person's mastered Grade-I and is in Grade-II.

And the *just* complacent, "Oh, well, I guess this is how it is" mentality, is something we treat at a more mundane level, when an individual is basically *agreeing* to these conditions that they are an *effect*—that Life is this thing that is happening *to* them, and all these things are happening *to* them, which kind of gives them reason or some kind of excuse to go about this "lower level" of operations thereafter.

And these are the types of things, again, that we are out to repair and resolve with our "beta-defragmentation" program.

It's a strange and esoteric sentiment to say an individual has "found" themselves or that we are on a pathway to "Self-discovery"; because, I mean, *who is doing the looking and discovering* if it isn't the Self. So... I mean, it seemed to me that the most aberrative effort a society could ever do to make or control confusion or fragmentation is to keep telling their population of humans that they need to spend the rest of their lives *finding* themselves.

Because, you could go and occupy your time "chasing your tail" for the rest of your existence, you know, just to come back to that point. So really, the idea behind working at "*self-processing*"—working through the material of Mardukite Systemology—is not so much a Self-*dis*-covery as a Self-*un*-covering *and* removing the layers—the artificial imprinting, the mental programming—and then understanding that Self is *not* any of the personalities or roles it has chosen to take on—whether it's this lifetime or other lifetimes.

Most of these "personality-program-packages"—they're assumed because of something that's happened. For example, an individual goes through one lifetime with a particular goal and they decide that they haven't reached that goal and they decide that the individuals that they've been in opposition to during that time-period is suddenly the personality-program to take on.

So, they come into—they come back basically trying to accomplish some goal, but they do it under some other personality or type, you know, and the next time... This just kind of keeps compounding and compounding. What we're trying to do is basically peel back these layers and get an individual back to *Self*—without the consideration or the limitations or the imprinting that's *attached to* these personalities.

Because, you know, rest assured—not only is experience a factor in fragmentation, but so is any "personality-program," any of these "phases" an individual takes on. Because there's other classifications that goes along with them —once an individual starts *identifying* that they *are* a "mother" or they *are* a "student" or they *are*... And they are applying and fixing the concept of "I-am" and they are fixing their "Beingness" or their point-of-view *to those* considerations—well, you know, there you have it; that's what's basically taking place.

And these aren't—none of these are ever Self; but they *are* particular "packages" *of* all of the stuff that you would "assume" in order to actually have an experience. So, you're basically going about your life having an experience, but you're looking at it through "mother-glasses"; or you're going through having an experience, but you're programmed to believe a "student" is supposed to think and behave a certain way, so you start doing *that.*

These are ways in which artificial "phases" actually inhibit the ability to actually experience *Life* for and as *Self.* So, then the idea that the individual is Self-directing control and responsibility of their experience of the Human Condition and executing *Will*—no matter what kind of Grades you've studied before; no matter what kind of rituals—the idea that the individual *believes* that they're Self-directing *Will* to its full potential while still residing in any find of state of beta-(fragmentation), is a *little bit "loopy."*

And so here, when we talk about the division between the "Master" and the "Wizard" levels—at the very least in Grade-III, we're talking about the Tarot Card: The Magician; we're talking about the actualization of the "Magician"—the one that's able to actualize an effective use of their *Will* in creating the *effects* in the world and having control over the Human experience.

Really, again, we kind of come full circle with Mardukite Systemology, because we're looking at the final "Mastery" and the *true* application of all the stuff that we've been kind of hinting around at since the very *first* course lecture—from the very first exploration of *what* "magic" *is*.

So, then, when we're talking about the *upper* points on the Standard Model—or the Alpha states, or what we're treating on the ZU-line—*exterior* to beta-existence, we're talking about the point of *Will* at "5.0" as basically the potential of actualization by the first order of understanding in beta-existence. By the first—basically, the idea that you're operating still within the Physical Existence; you're basically applying efforts of *Will* still *to* parameters of beta-existence, and *beyond* that though, we work to basically eliminate this idea that beta-existence is *all* that there is—and that there are other considerations for occupying a Universe.

Above the application of *Will*—you know, we've talked a little bit about Alpha-Thought—but, the point of *Games* and *Logics* and other *Universes* are realized into being is at "6.0"; and this is the potential for the *second order* of understanding. We talked about the various levels of understanding—the various levels of knowledge—as far as Grades *One*, *Two* and *Three*; well, we see how these actually apply within the sphere of our understanding at a Master level. Where we are talking about applying *efforts* to physical existence with *Will*—we're still talking about a first level/order of understanding; because we're talking about dealing with parameters that are already there—dealing with change or affecting the Physical Universe.

But at "6.0" we're talking about the idea of dealing in strictly (the) realizations of higher points of Awareness, where an individual can actually create—create pretty much anything. You know, we talk about the limitlessness of the "astral" or the "Mind" or the "spiritual realm" or what not; this is where we find that—because the point of the Alpha-Spirit on the Standard Model on the ZU-line is "7.0," which we consider *total* Self-Actualization as the Alpha-State; the basic state an individual was before any (other) considerations.

Of course, *that's* our aim from the third and highest order of realization and understanding, which is—you know, we start dealing with "spiritual consciousness" or "Cosmic Consciousness"—all of these upper-level things in Mardukite Systemology. So, in that same "three tiered" concept of the first three orders of understanding, the first three levels of realization, the first three Grades and so forth—we see a refinement of the same principles of Cosmic Manifestation repeating themselves at higher levels.

We express very firmly that *Will* at "5.0" is Self-Awareness directing Alpha Thought from "6.0" into a creative expression below "5.0" as it's going to manifest; we're basically sending it down this channel or path in order to essentially be the *cause* of some *effect*; and so the Self as Alpha-Spirit at "7.0" is the *cause* of *Will* at "5.0" and then when we're dealing with its application or its point of control and command of the (Mind-System), the Master Control Center at "4.0" becomes the effect of the *cause* as *Will*, and then is directing as *cause* down to lower systems.

And so this is why we call it a "Systemology," because we're dealing with a systematic understanding of the relay of energy—all the way in between Self and the experiences *as* Self in this physical existence; and the refinement of that—how it operates and how an individual can remain at *cause* and basically be in command of this experience.

Far and beyond the idea that—you know, from the Mardukite Master Course and Mardukite Systemology—that a Seeker is just kinda gonna grow wings and fly away... The real idea behind it was to establish a greater point of certainty for all the esoteric knowledge and all the material that's been established over the last *twenty-five* years; but also to get somebody to be able to play a better *Game*—to have a better experience of being Self-directed as involved in the Human Condition in this lifetime.

Really, I mean, to pursue anything farther—let's at least get to that point and see where they're at... you know? They've discovered—an individual—their level of certainty and Self-direction toward the accomplishment of any future goals, or overcoming future challenges or barriers—solving problems. This is really linked closely to the types of beliefs and imprinting maintained about all their past and present successes and failures.

As more failed and unrealized goals begin to stack up, they become a source of fragmentation; and so you find tendencies where an individual as present—you know, we talk about the neurotic—their present time situations; they're just not able to deal with, so they're constantly looping back into these mental patterns in regards to anything taking place around them. So, everything—anything that happens is suddenly a "huge" challenge. Well, such an individual is obviously not going to be able to look to trying to make goals or accomplish anything in the future—or reach beyond where they already are; because they're just too busy stumbling around with that.

Obviously, an individual that's still reliving some kind of past experience or projecting something that's taken place in the past as being what's taking place now, and only applying that level of awareness and reasoning to it—that individual probably isn't going to do very well either, in terms of getting along in life.

So, at the very least, I mean—you know, we're not looking to anything too "supernatural" here; I haven't made any "great" claims or promises, even though we've been dealing with 6,000 years of esoterica; we've been talking about all manners of "magic" and "witchcraft" and "Druidry" and "mental ability" and so on and so forth—all we've really been doing is treating a baseline level of understanding with this, so an individual just doesn't walk around carrying the great "Mystery" of it.

We've been able to illuminate—during the course of this, and all these materials, all these lectures, the whole scope of this—6,000 years of not only underground tradition and underground esoteric spirituality, but also the history and development *of* Human civilization and how we've reach the point that we've gotten to. And I mean, this is a pretty critical component for understanding the relationship that Self —particularly whatever conditions have been assumed or considered for Self—has with the environment; the setting that's taking place around.

What we find is, you know—when we talk about an individual that's well adjusted; I mean, we talk about those that are successful—when we talk about those that have been a master of their craft, or those that have reached high pinnacles in terms of the occult sciences, or even now our endeavors in Mardukite Systemology—we're talking about the ability to, basically, handle and manage the Human Condition in a way that really has never been treated before; it's only been hinted at. It's been strived for and then abandoned by countless philosophies, physical sciences; it's been referred to for thousands of years in all these various esoteric and occult and magical schools—and, you know, finally now... Still yet from the underground, yet to become hugely known or widely publicized—but the work of Mardukite Zuism, the work of the Systemology Society, delivering a higher benchmark and greater state of *Beingness* in which to work and operate this *Knowingness* —because these points have not been reached prior.

This is new ground that we have charted. We took the foundations from thousands of years of work. We took what we knew we could stand upon—we took what we knew would hold some water—and we developed it, we refined it; we've been able to bring it to a level, now, of understanding that surpasses anything that has taken place in the past. We've been able to deliver a "Course" to essentially *match* the level of duplication; if an individual was practicing or working with us at the Mardukite Academy, or any kind of direct level of apprenticeship.

So, this is where we are at—this is what the Mardukite Master Course has culminated—this is the whole purpose behind it. I hope you've been able to achieve something of some benefit—something that's been discussed, if not being able to take the whole scope with you, something within this last several weeks of intensive examination of all these various materials—that it has done something for you.

And so, at this juncture—I mean... There's very little more for me to do than to hand out these certificates [*laughs*] and basically call it "done." You've been able to get through now, *forty-eight* lectures; we've covered *twenty-five* years of material; *3,600* pages of textbook. You've been able to reach a point of practical application with this that is probably unparalleled in most of the other "How-To" books and other things on the "New Age" market. So, this is the point where I basically set you *loose* and see what you'll be able to do—what you'll be able to develop. Certainly this isn't the *end* of the "courses"—this isn't the end of the development of the work. But, we've reached a point where we have a Master-level of understanding; a Master-level of realization on all of this material, so...

At this juncture, I *charge you* with the *wisdom of serpents* and the *harmlessness of doves*; and send you forth in this world as *wolves* among *sheep.*

Go *shine* and make us proud!

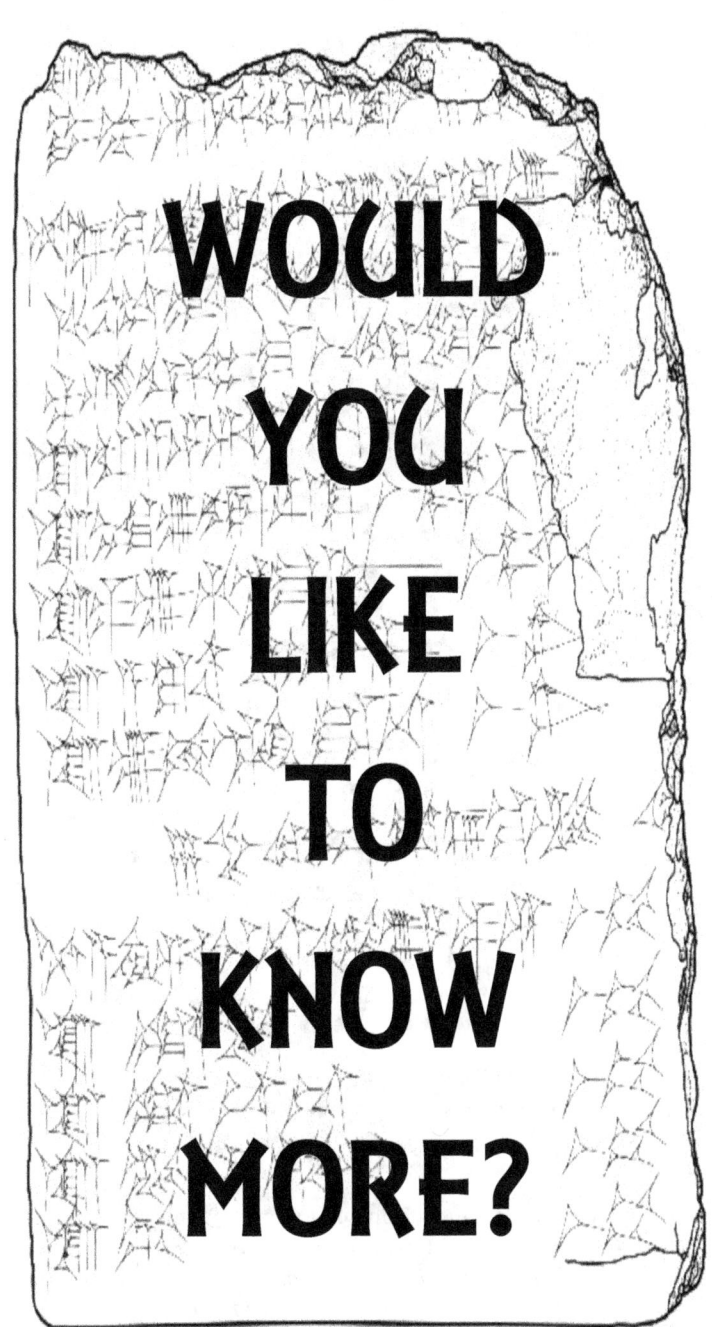

AVAILABLE FROM THE **JOSHUA FREE** PUBLISHING IMPRINT

*The Original Mardukite Master Course Lecture Volumes!
Experience the Legendary Course From Anywhere
in the Universe—Available in Four Volumes!*

MAGICK & MYSTICISM
The Academy Lectures – Vol. I

DRUIDS, ELVES & DRAGONS
The Academy Lectures – Vol. II

MESOPOTAMIAN TRADITION
The Academy Lectures – Vol. III

Based on the lectures by Joshua Free

*Transcripts of the Mardukite Master Course Academy Lectures
given at the Mardukite Academy in September 2020.*

This is part of a four-part series, each volume providing a serious Seeker with transcripts to 12 of the 48 Academy Lectures previously published in the mega-anthology "*Complete Mardukite Master Course.*"

Each volume is designed to match the correlating Master Edition textbook, such as "*Great Magickal Arcanum,*" "*Merlyn's Complete Book of Druidism,*" "*Necronomicon: The Complete Anunnaki Legacy*" and "*Systemology Handbook.*"

AVAILABLE FROM THE **JOSHUA FREE** PUBLISHING IMPRINT

SYSTEMOLOGY
The Pathway to Self-Honesty
ORIGINAL UNDERGROUND INTRODUCTIONS
REVISED AND REISSUED IN HARDCOVER

SYSTEMOLOGY
The Original Thesis of Mardukite New Thuoght
by Joshua Free
(Mardukite Systemology Liber-S-1X)

The very first underground discourses released to the "New Thought" division of the Mardukite Research Organization privately over a decade ago and providing the inspiration for rapid futurist spiritual technology called "Mardukite Systemology."

THE POWER OF ZU
Applying Mardukite Zuism & Systemology to Everyday Life
by Joshua Free
Foreword by Reed Penn
(Mardukite Systemology Liber-S-1Z)

A unique introductory course on Mardukite Zuism & Systemology, including transcripts from a 3-day lecture series given by Joshua Free in December 2019 to launch the Mardukite Academy of Systemology & Founding Church of Mardukite Zuism just in time for the 2020's.

WOULD YOU LIKE TO KNOW MORE ???

Take your first steps on the

SYSTEMOLOGY
Pathway to Self-Honesty

with the book that started it all!

Rediscover the original system of perfecting the Human Condition on a Pathway that leads to Infinity. Here is a way!—a map to chart spiritual potential and redefine the future of what it means to be human.

A landmark public debut of Grade-III Systemology and foundation stone for reaching higher and taking back control of your

DESTINY

(*Mardukite Systemology Grade-III Research Volume, Liber-One*)

AVAILABLE FROM THE **JOSHUA FREE** PUBLISHING IMPRINT

SYSTEMOLOGY
The Pathway to Self-Honesty

CRYSTAL CLEAR

(Handbook for Seekers)

Self-Actualization and Spiritual Ascension in This Lifetime

by Joshua Free

Mardukite Systemology Grade-III, Liber-2B

Revised Edition

available exclusively as an Academy Collector's Hardcover Edition

Take control of your destiny and chart the first steps
toward your own spiritual evolution.
Realize new potentials of the Human Condition with
a Self-guiding handbook for Self-Processing
toward Self-Actualization in Self-Honesty using actual
techniques and training provided for the coveted
"Mardukite Self-Defragmentation Course Program"
—once only available directly and privately from the
underground International Systemology Society.

Discover the amazing power behind the
applied spiritual technology
used for counseling and advisement in
the Mardukite Zuism tradition.

(Revised Second Edition Now Available!)

AVAILABLE FROM THE **JOSHUA FREE** PUBLISHING IMPRINT

SYSTEMOLOGY
The Pathway to Self-Honesty

SYSTEMOLOGY HANDBOOK

The ultimate operator's manual to the Human Condition and unlocking the true power of the Spirit.

** *"Modern Mardukite Zuism"* **
** *"The Tablets of Destiny"* **
** *"Crystal Clear"* **
** *"The Power of ZU"* **
** *"Systemology—Original Thesis"* **
** *Human, More Than Human* **
** *Defragmentation* **
** *Patterns & Cycles* **
** *Transhuman Generations* **

(Complete Grade-III Master Edition Anthology)

AVAILABLE FROM THE **JOSHUA FREE** PUBLISHING IMPRINT

MARDUKITE MASTER COURSE
Keys to the Gates of Higher Understanding

Now you can experience the Legendary "Master Course" from anywhere in the Universe, exactly as given in person by Joshua Free to the "Mardukite Academy of Systemology" in September 2020.

800+ pages of materials collected in this volume provide Seekers with full transcripts to all *48 Academy Lectures* of the legendary *"Mardukite Master Course"* combined with all course outlines, supplements and critical handouts from the original *"Instructor's Manual"*—making this the most complete definitive single-source delivery of New Age understanding and spiritual technology.

Referencing 25 years of research, development and publishing, including *"Necronomicon: The Complete Anunnaki Legacy,"* *"The Great Magickal Arcanum," "The Systemology Handbook"* and *"Merlyn's Complete Book of Druidism."*

AVAILABLE FROM THE **JOSHUA FREE** PUBLISHING IMPRINT

SYSTEMOLOGY
The Gateways to Infinity

METAHUMAN DESTINATIONS

Piloting the Course to Homo Novus

Written by Joshua Free
Foreword by David Zibert

Mardukite Systemology Grade-IV Metahumanism Professional Pilot Course, Liber-Two

exclusively available in a hardcover premiere first edition

Drawing from the "Arcane Tablets" and nearly a year of additional research, experimentation and workshops since the introduction of applied spiritual technology and systematic processing methods, Joshua Free provides the ground-breaking manual for those seeking to correct—or "defragment"—the conditions that have trapped viewpoints of the Spirit into programming and encoding of the Human Condition.

Experience the revolutionary professional course in advanced spiritual technology for Mardukite Systemologists to "Pilot" the way to higher ideals that can free us from the Human Condition and return ultimate command and control of creation to the Spirit.

(Includes Grade-IV Liber-2C, Liber-2D and Liber-3C)

AVAILABLE FROM THE **JOSHUA FREE** PUBLISHING IMPRINT

SYSTEMOLOGY
The Gateways to Infinity

IMAGINOMICON

Accessing the Gateway to Higher Universes

A New Grimoire for the Human Spirit

by Joshua Free

Mardukite Systemology Grade-IV Metahumanism, Wizard Level-0, Liber-3D

available in both as premiere hardcover or revised collector's edition

The Way Out. Hidden for 6,000 Years.
But now we've found the Key.
A grimore to summon and invoke, command and control,
the most powerful spirit to ever exist.
Your Self.

Access beyond physical existence.
Fly free across all Gateways.
Go back to where it all began and reclaim that
personal universe which the *Spirit* once called "*Home.*"

Break free from the Matrix;
command the Mind and control the Body
from outside those systems
— because *You* were never "human" —
fully realize what it means to be a *spiritual being*,
then rise up through the Gateways to Higher Universes
and *BE.*

AVAILABLE FROM THE **JOSHUA FREE** PUBLISHING IMPRINT

SYSTEMOLOGY
Gateways to Infinite Self-Honesty

THE WAY OF THE WIZARD
(Utilitarian Systemology)
A New Metahuman Ethic
by Joshua Free

The Systemology Society Beta-Defragmentation Booster
and stabilizer for upper-level Wizard Grades.
Based on the "Freedom From" Grade-IV lecture series
given by Joshua Free in July 2021 at Mardukite Academy
and developmental research for the remaining year.

Accumulated involvement in dangerous situations, states of
confusion, unjust destruction and being at the effect end of faulty
—or blatantly false—information, all lend to fragmented purposes
that are non-survival (or counter-survival) oriented, leading us
away from routes to achieve "greater heights"—higher more ideal
states of Knowing and Beingness—including the
"Magic Universe" preceding this one.

(Mardukite Systemology Grade-IV-V Bridge, Liber-Three/3E)

THE MARDUKITE RESEARCH LIBRARY ARCHIVE COLLECTION

AVAILABLE FROM THE **JOSHUA FREE** PUBLISHING IMPRINT

Necronomicon: The Anunnaki Bible : 10th Anniversary Collector's
Edition—LIBER-N,L,G,9+W-M+S (*Hardcover*)

*Gates of the Necronomicon : The Secret Anunnaki Tradition of
Babylon :* 10th Anniversary Collector's Edition—
LIBER-50,51/52,R+555 (*Hardcover*)

*Necronomicon—The Anunnaki Grimoire : A Manual of Practical
Babylonian Magick :* 10th Anniversary Collector's Edition—
LIBER-E,W/Z,M+K (*Hardcover*)

The Complete Anunnaki Bible: A Source Book of Esoteric Archaeology
—LIBER-N,L,G,9+W-M+S (*Hardcover and Paperback*)

*Anunnaki Bible : The Cuneiform Scriptures—New Standard
Zuist Edition :* Abridged Pocket Version (*Hardcover & Paperback*)

*Sumerian Religion : Introducing the Anunnaki Gods of Mesopotamian
Neopaganism :* 10th Anniv. Collector's Ed.—LIBER-50 (*Hardcover*)

*Babylonian Myth & Magic : Anunnaki Mysticism of Mesopotamian
Neopaganism :* 10th Anniv. Coll. Ed.—LIBER-51+E (*Hardcover*)

*The Complete Book of Marduk by Nabu : A Pocket Anunnaki
Devotional Companion to Babylonian Prayers & Rituals :*
10th Anniversary Collector's Edition—LIBER-W+Z (*Hardcover*)

*The Maqlu Ritual Book : A Pocket Companion to Babylonian
Exorcisms, Banishing Rites & Protective Spells :*
10th Anniversary Collector's Edition—LIBER-M (*Hardcover*)

*Novem Portis: Necronomicon Revelations & Nine Gates of the Kingdom
of Shadows :* 10th Anniv. Collector's Ed.—LIBER-R+9 (*Hardcover*)

*Elvenomicon—or—Secret Traditions of Elves & Faeries : Elven Magick
& Druid Lore :* 15th Anniv. Collector's Ed.—LIBER-D (*Hardcover*)

Draconomicon : The Book of Ancient Dragon Magick
25th Anniversary Collector's Edition—LIBER-D3 (*Hardcover*)

The Druid's Handbook : Ancient Magick for a New Age
20th Anniversary Collector's Edition—LIBER-D2 (*Hardcover*)

The Sorcerer's Handbook : A Complete Guide to Practical Magick
21st Anniversary Collector's Edition—(*Hardcover*)

The Witch's Handbook : A Complete Grimoire of Witchcraft
21st Anniversary Collector's Edition—(*Hardcover*)

The Vampyre's Handbook : Secret Rites of Modern Vampires
5th Anniversary Collector's Edition—LIBER V1+V2 (*Hardcover*)

∞

SILVER ANNIVERSARY

19 95   20 20

JOSHUA FREE

PUBLISHED BY THE **JOSHUA FREE** IMPRINT REPRESENTING

**The Founding Church of Mardukite Zuism
& Mardukite Academy of Systemology**

mardukite.com

www.ingramcontent.com/pod-product-compliance
Lightning Source LLC
Chambersburg PA
CBHW070742060526
44119CB00070B/73